A WORLD BANK COUNTRY STUDY

Korea
The Management of External Liabilities

The World Bank
Washington, D.C., U.S.A.

World Bank Country Studies are reports originally prepared for internal use as part of the continuing analysis by the Bank of the economic and related conditions of its developing member countries and of its dialogues with the governments. Some of the reports are published informally with the least possible delay for the use of governments and the academic, business and financial, and development communities. Thus, the typescript has not been prepared in accordance with the procedures appropriate to formal printed texts, and the World Bank accepts no responsibility for errors.

Any maps that accompany the text have been prepared solely for the convenience of readers. The designations and presentation of material in them do not imply the expression of any opinion whatsoever on the part of the World Bank, its affiliates, or its Board or member countries concerning the legal status of any country, territory, city, or area or of the authorities thereof or concerning the delimitation of its boundaries or its national affiliation.

The most recent World Bank publications are described in the catalog *New Publications*, a new edition of which is issued in the spring and fall of each year. The complete backlist of publications is shown in the annual *Index of Publications*, which contains an alphabetical title list and indexes of subjects, authors, and countries and regions; it is of value principally to libraries and institutional purchasers. The latest edition of each of these is available free of charge from the Publications Sales Unit, Department F, The World Bank, 1818 H Street, N.W., Washington, D.C. 20433, U.S.A., or from Publications, The World Bank, 66 avenue d'Iéna, 75116 Paris, France.

Library of Congress Cataloging-in-Publication Data

```
Korea : the management of external liabilities.
        p.   cm. -- (A World Bank country study)
    Bibliography: p.
    Includes index.
    ISBN 0-8213-1026-7
    1. Investments, Foreign--Korea (South) 2. Loans, Foreign--Korea
(South)   I. International Bank for Reconstruction and Development.
II. Series.
HG5780.5.A3K65 1988
336.3'4'095195--dc19                                    87-37194
                                                           CIP
```

Abstract

This report assesses the structure of Korea's external
liabilities in the light of general principles of liability
management, current and anticipated country-specific
characteristics, and developments in international capital
markets. While stressing that neither the level nor the
composition of Korea's external liabilities poses an
immediate problem, the Report notes deficiencies with
respect to the sharing of risk, the correlation of debt
service with ability to pay and the diversification of
sources of financing which could present difficulties in
future periods of foreign exchange scarcity and economic
stagnation. It notes that Korea could take advantage of
emerging opportunities in international capital markets to
overcome these deficiencies by giving preference to bonds
and equities over loans in future external financing
arrangements and by encouraging private non-guaranteed debt
instead of public debt. It argues that such actions are
consistent with Korea's evolving needs as well as with
lender preferences, and will provide Korea a status within
the international financial community commensurate with its
status in the world industrial community.

CURRENCY EQUIVALENTS
(January 1987)

Currency unit	=	Won
US$1	=	W 860
W 100	=	US$0.12
W 1,000,000	=	US$1,163

GLOSSARY OF ABBREVIATIONS

ADRs	–	American Depository Receipts
CP	–	Commercial Paper
DFI	–	Direct Foreign Investment
ECP	–	EuroCommercial Paper Program
IFC	–	International Finance Corporation
KEB	–	Korea Exchange Bank
KDB	–	Korea Development Bank
KEXIM	–	Korea Export Import Bank
KSE	–	Korea Stock Exchange
KSFC	–	Korea Securities Finance Corporation
KSDA	–	Korea Securities Dealers Association
MOF	–	Ministry of Finance
NIF	–	Note Issuance Facility
OTC	–	Over the Counter
PFI	–	Portfolio Foreign Investment
RUF	–	Revolving Underwriting Facility
SEC	–	Securities Exchange Commission
SSB	–	Securities Supervisory Board
TLI	–	Transferable Loan Instrument
VTR	–	Video Tape Recorder

KOREA

EXTERNAL LIABILITY MANAGEMENT

Table of Contents

This report was written by Farrukh Iqbal on the basis of background reports prepared by L. Ahamed, K. Stephenson (Bank Staff) and A. Grimes and N. McEvoy (Consultants). Additional material and assessments of Korea's current and prospective access to international capital markets were obtained through a visit to Seoul, Tokyo, Hong Kong and London during May 23 - July 7, 1986. The support provided by M. Phair of the International Finance Corporation and by officials of the Ministry of Finance, Economic Planning Board, Korea Development Bank and Korea Exchange Bank is gratefully acknowledged.

List of Tables

Executive Summary

1.   This Report assesses the structure of Korea's external liabilities in the light of general principles of liability management, current and anticipated country-specific characteristics, and developments in international capital markets. An examination of Korea's current external liability structure indicates that neither the level nor the composition of such liabilities poses an immediate problem. On the contrary Korea currently enjoys a rather comfortable external financing environment characterized by an excess supply of funds and improvements in terms and conditions. Nevertheless, being a very open economy, Korea is vulnerable to external shocks, and some features of Korea's external liability structure could generate problems for the country in future periods of foreign exchange scarcity and economic stagnation. Current market conditions are propitious for Korea to reexamine its external liability structure in a long-term perspective and undertake measures with respect to its external financing arrangements that should improve its ability to absorb and deflect future shocks that may emanate from the international economic system.

2.   Decisions regarding the composition of future foreign capital inflows into Korea must be undertaken in the light of several ongoing developments. First, Government has been gradually withdrawing from active intervention in the allocation of credit and investment in the economy. As a result, the implicit guarantee of open credit lines (and Government "bailouts") can no longer to be taken for granted by the Korean corporate sector. Corporate finance decisions, whether they involve domestic or foreign funding, must take this development into account. Second, Korea's industrial structure is changing towards industries which are inherently riskier, require more marketing knowledge and face export market uncertainty because of protectionism. This, too, has implications for corporate financing decisions, especially with regard to the use of foreign equity investment.

3.   Third, lender preferences for foreign capital instruments are changing. These preferences are expressed in the emerging trend towards "securitisation" in the international financial markets and involve a shift in capital flows away from bank lending towards marketable debt instruments (such as floating rate notes) and equities. Indeed, the distinction between bond and equity markets is becoming blurred and there has developed a considerable demand for hybrid securities (such as convertible debentures). In addition, technical innovations (such as currency and interest rate swaps) have occurred in the market which permit both borrowers and lenders a wider range of opportunities to achieve desired asset and liability structures.

Assessment of Korea's External Liability Structure

4.   It is generally agreed that in addition to low cost the following are desirable objectives for the structure of a country's external liabilities: (a) a maturity profile that allows a wide dispersal of repayment over time; (b) diversified currency composition; (c) a sharing of risk between

borrowers and lenders; (d) a dispersal of risk inside the economy; (e) a correlation between debt service and the ability to pay, and (f) a diversified lender or investor base. An assessment of Korea's external liability structure in terms of the above characteristics shows that the most notable deficiencies occur with respect to the sharing of risk, the correlation of debt service with the country's ability to pay and diversification of the sources of financing. Each of these deficiencies can be overcome by obtaining external financing in the form of equity rather than debt. A major conclusion, therefore, is that Korea should seek to obtain an increasing proportion of its future external finance in the form of portfolio and direct foreign investment.

5.   <u>Maturity Structure</u>. Korea's short-term debt has declined steadily as a proportion of total debt since 1983 and now stands at about 20%. Short-term debt is now equivalent to about 3.5 months of imports, a fairly safe level by conventional standards. Thus, Korea's debt maturity structure is quite sound at present. Nevertheless, there is no harm in lengthening maturities should it be possible to do so at reasonable cost. Such an opportunity appears to be available under present market conditions, especially given the context of Korea's excellent economic fundamentals (see paras. 1.09-1.11).

6.   <u>Currency Composition</u>. The currency composition of Korea's debt (80% US dollars, 12.5% Japanese yen) is reasonably balanced from the point of view of the currency composition of its export receipts. To the extent, however, that the relative importance of the US as a destination for Korean exports may decline in the future as Korea pursues trade diversification and/or if trade frictions with the US intensify, it would be useful to diversify into non-dollar OECD currencies. Diversification away from the dollar would be justified also from a pure hedging point of view because of the presently heavy representation of the dollar in Korea's debt. Diversification would probably also be suggested by the application of the principle that variations in the cost of debt-servicing should as far as possible be offset by changes in Korea's ability to pay as measured by its terms of trade. However, decisions regarding currency composition must also take into account the likely direction of future exchange rate movements. For example, a substantial shift into non-dollar obligations might not be desirable until such time as the prospects for dollar depreciation become dim. At any rate, given the increased volatility of exchange rates and Korea's sensitivity to terms of trade, it would be desirable for Korea to adopt an active currency management strategy in the future. Such a strategy would involve (i) tapping different capital markets directly or (ii) arranging currency swaps if direct access should not be possible (see paras. 1.12-1.17).

7.   <u>Project Risk Sharing</u>. At present about 95% of foreign capital inflow into Korea is in the form of bank loans and bonds. With such general obligation finance the downside risk of project failure is borne entirely by the borrower. Since most Korean borrowing is, for all practical purposes, at sovereign risk, this places a rather heavy burden on Government. If Government is to extricate itself from intervention in the market economy, it must encourage a greater amount of risk sharing between foreign lenders and domestic corporate borrowers. This can be done by encouraging the inflow of both direct and portfolio foreign investment. In recent years initiatives have

been taken by Government to enhance such foreign equity flows and the response has been quite encouraging. Further initiatives are planned under the ongoing liberalization program. It is recommended that advantage be taken of the exceptionally favorable current outlook for direct and portfolio foreign investment and the pace of liberalization be quickened (see paras. 1.18-1.20).

8.   Dispersal of Risk. At present 90% of Korea's external debt is covered by government guarantees. While such gurantees have resulted in better borrowing terms and enhanced access to external finance for public and private Korean borrowers they have the disadvantage of (a) encouraging excessive risk-taking by both borrowers and lenders; (b) involving Government too deeply in industrial investment decisions; and (c) placing a potentially large financial burden on Government. All these disadvantages have been evident in the recent experience of the Korean construction and shipping industries in which firms grew recklessly on the strength of (explicit or implicit) Government-guranteed credit and had to be bailed-out and restructured when slumping demand for their outputs exposed their financial weaknesses. (see paras. 1.22-1.23). In the long run it would be beneficial to have a wider distribution of default risk within the economy. This can be done by encouraging a shift from public to private non-guaranteed debt and by encouraging the replacement of debt by equity.

9.   Correlation Between Debt Service and Ability to Pay. Korea's highly unbalanced external liability structure (95% debt, 5% equity) fails to provide it with a hedge since debt-service obligations are inflexible and bear little correlation with the country's ability to pay. Korea's openness and the size and nature of its debt ($45 billion with about 60% at floating rates) make it vulnerable to even small changes in the international trade and finance environment. In view of the importance of the external sector to Korea's economic welfare, it would appear useful to pursue external financing arrangements whose servicing obligations are pro-cyclically related to the country's ability to pay.

10.   Perhaps the most appropriate instruments for this are equity investments. It is generally observed that the annual service payments associated with direct foreign investment are more correlated with movements in national income than are debt service payments. The same is the case with portfolio foreign investment for which dividend pay-out rates and share prices tend to fluctuate pro-cyclically with national income. A potential instrument that would also possess this particular characteristic of linking repayments to ability to pay is the trade-linked bond. Such a bond would offer a return linked to the value of Korea's exports or, perhaps more realistically, to a generally accepted index of world trade growth. Such a bond has not appeared in the market yet and there may be considerable technical difficulties in bringing it to market. Nevertheless, it is an attractive possibility. It would permit a close correspondence between debt service payments and export revenues, thus reducing Korea's vulnerability to external disturbances. Such an instrument would appeal to the same investors who are attracted by Korean equities since it would be similar in many respects to a mutual fund comprised of the stocks of major export-oriented conglomerates. Korea's debt managers may find it worthwhile to explore the market for such a bond; it may be an acceptable alternative to faster internationalization of the Korean equities market (see paras. 1.24-1.28; 2.46).

11.   Diversification of Sources. A secure flow of external finance facilitates the planning process, permits the smooth utilization of real resources, avoids disruptive balance of payments adjustment and maintains debt servicing capacity. One way to enhance the stability of foreign capital inflows is to diversify as much as possible among sources of financing, both geographically and by type of instrument. This is especially important for Korea because its external liabilities are extremely concentrated in the form of bank loans provided by Japanese and American commercial banks. Significant difficulties would ensue if these sources were to become less accommodating in the future as a result of economic or political frictions or unforeseen events external to Korea. Instrument diversification could be achieved by increasing the rate of substitution of bank credits with such forms of financing as international bonds and direct and portfolio investment. Geographical diversification would involve tapping as many capital markets as possible and targeting a wide range of investor groups within each market (see paras. 1.29-1.30).

Elements of Desirable External Financing Strategy for Korea

12.   If the objectives of risk sharing, correlation of servicing with ability to pay, and diversification of sources of funding are accorded high priority in Korea's future plans it would follow that the future inflow of foreign capital into Korea should be largely in the form of equity instruments. In the short run, however, such a financial strategy would not achieve significant modification of the external liability structure since the existing pattern of capital inflows into Korea is overwhelmingly debt-oriented. Despite the many perceived problems with general obligation financing, it is difficult to foresee a rapid shift away from the dominance of syndicated bank loans and floating rate bonds. Furthermore, as far as portfolio investments are concerned, it will take time for Korea's absorption capacity to be sufficiently enlarged (through promotion and reform of the stock market) so as to permit such investments to play a significant role in external liability management. These observations have consequences for a future strategy for external financing: in the short-run efforts should be concentrated on adjusting the existing array of instruments to bring them more into line with the desirable inflow characteristics; this would involve giving preference to bonds over loans in financing arrangements and encouraging private non-guaranteed debt instead of public debt; in the longer run, however, it should be recognized that the existing external liability structure is not immutable and efforts should be made to increase the proportion of equity in foreign capital inflows.

13.   The main elements that would characterize a desirable future external financing strategy for Korea within this framework are discussed below.

14.   Bond Market Strategy. Korea should continue to substitute bond financing for syndicated credits but should attempt to exploit the bond market's potential to a fuller extent. International bond markets hold considerable promise for a country in Korea's position provided they are approached strategically with clear long-term goals in mind rather than opportunistically with a view to making the cheapest short-term deals. Among bond market instruments floating rate notes (FRNs) warrant attention because they can be

superior to syndicated credits, hitherto Korea's most heavily used instrument, in terms of cost, maturity and diversity of investor base. The cost of FRN's is likely to remain below that of syndicated credits because of their marketability (or liquidity) and the fact that syndicated loan makers (i.e. banks) are being affected by higher capital-asset requirements and deposit interest rate deregulation. The potential liquidity of bonds also enables longer maturities to be established since a wider group of investors, and not just banks, are potential buyers and a broader range of buyer-preference exists. The wider investor base also offers the potential for greater diversification among sources of funds (see paras. 2.37-2.40).

15.   Public Borrowing. How bond market potential is exploited depends partly on the situation and partly on the strategy of the issuer. To date, Korea's experience, especially in the Eurobond market, has not been satisfactory in terms of maturities and diversification. While some reasons for this experience are to be found in Korea's tight economic situation in the early 1980s, the illiquidity and narrow holding of Korean paper has also been due to the Korean practice of coming to the market many times with small issues, of preferring cost over other desirable characteristics in most deals, of avoiding issues in the name of the Government and of not emphasizing the importance of marketing and presentation to the extent necessary for a relatively new participant.

16.   A bond market strategy that would stand the best chance of overcoming the present perception of Korean sovereign or "semi-sovereign" paper should contain the following elements:

(a) Large Size of Issue: The size of typical future bond issues should be large, say a minimum of $250 million, so as to generate liquidity in the secondary market. Dealers need to maintain inventories of each issue in order to effectively make markets in these issues. There are, however, considerable economies of scale in the holding of inventories and thus large issues do better than small issues. In this context it is also worth noting that the size of swap-related issues needs to be quite large in order to make the swap worthwhile to all participants.

(b) Marketing. Korea should engage in a major marketing effort to attract the interest of international money managers and to overcome their imperfect knowledge of Korea's economic and political situation. The marketing effort should also identify lead managers who have a good track record of non-bank placements. The greatest potential would initially appear to be in the Japanese market, but the European, especially the Swiss, markets also warrant further consideration. Now that Korea's economic situation has taken a sharp turn for the better, presenting Korea's case to the financial community should be easier and should generate high returns.

17.   Private versus Public Debt. The sharp improvement in Korea's economic prospects occasioned by the decline in the price of oil and the appreciation of the yen relative to the won heralds new opportunities for Korea in international capital markets. Korea now anticipates sizable balance of

payments surpluses over the near future and its major private corporations are now in a position to establish significant market shares and brand-name presence in OECD markets. As a result the need for public or semi-public borrowing for balance of payments purposes is declining while the prospects of Korean corporations being able to borrow in their own names, and without government guarantees, are improving. The opportunity exists, therefore, for Korea to encourage a shift from public debt towards private non-guaranteed debt. This would have the benefits of dispersing default-risk away from the Government and increasing the familiarity of Korean corporate names in international capital markets. Towards this end Government should encourage private borrowers to adopt financial management, accounting and disclosure practices that will help them in converting their bright economic prospects into enhanced access to external finance. Any marketing effort undertaken to promote the semi-public names can also have positive spillover effects for private Korean corporate names. The recent assignment of favorable credit ratings to Korean sovereign risk by Moody's and S&P also bodes well for private Korean names although the advantage is more likely to be perceived in short and medium term financing arrangements then in access to long-term funds.

18.   <u>Short and Medium Term Financing</u>. Good opportunities exist for both public and private Korean entities to expand access to short and medium term financing at better terms than available through standard syndicated credits while, at the same time, diversifying away from bank finance (see paras. 2.25-2.29).

   (a) <u>Euronotes</u>: The Euronote market which offers very attractive medium-term financing in the form of underwritten note issuance facilities should be further explored. Recent forays by Korean entities into this market have been successful and Korea's sharply improved economic prospects can only make access better. The substantial presence in this market of corporations should make it possible to reduce reliance on bank finance.

   (b) <u>Commercial Paper</u>: The commercial paper (CP) markets in both Europe and the US can also be profitably explored. In the past Korea had limited access to these markets because of the lack of a US credit rating. Korean corporate names could only issue in the US CP market, for example, on the strength of a letter of credit guarantee by US banks. The recent acquisition of US credit ratings should open up international short-term finance markets to Korean paper to a greater extent and at lower cost than is presently the case. There exist large numbers of investors in both the US and European CP markets who are restricted by regulation, prospectus or custom from buying non-rated paper.

19.   <u>Swaps</u>: Korea should also continue altering the currency and interest-type mix of its liabilities through the use of swaps. For example Korea has virtually no direct access to fixed-rate US or Eurodollar facilities but has excellent access to fixed and floating rate yen facilities. It should consider trading on its comparative advantage and swap some of its floating rate yen or dollar liabilities into fixed rate ones. Of course, the timing of

swaps should be carefully considered since terms and conditions vary from day to day. What is being recommended here is that an active currency management strategy be adopted as part of the overall debt management program. Appropriately conceived and timed swaps can help Korea diversify its sources of finance as well as lower its currency and interest rate risk (see paras. 2.47-2.54).

20.   **Convertible Debentures**: Advantage should be taken of the current market preference for hybrid securities in general and the strong interest in Korean convertible debentures in particular. The three issues floated so far have met with an enthusiastic response despite their carrying terms which were very favorable to the issuers. Further issues should be encouraged and the program of equity market liberalization in this particular regard should be accelerated to take advantage of market conditions. Bonds with equity warrants attached are also an attractive possibility. Since Korean equities are in high demand it would be opportune to include them in bond packages in such a way as to benefit from that demand. Further action in this area would be consistent with Korea's need to redress both the public-private and debt-equity imbalances in its liability structure.

21.   **Equity Enhancement Strategy**: Korea can take the following measures to increase the inflow of equity investment (see paras. 3.31-3.43 and paras. 4.12-4.14):

(a) expand existing investment funds for foreigners to purchase Korean stocks;

(b) establish additional funds, similar to the Korea Fund, on other foreign stock exchanges;

(c) accelerate the program of opening further industries for direct foreign investment;

(d   increase the limit under which automatic approval is granted for direct foreign investment;

(e) strengthen the domestic capital market by undertaking a number of technical, fiscal, institutional and market-promoting measures; and

(f) increase confidence in the domestic capital market by undertaking a number of reforms to improve corporate disclosure and accounting practices, to curb insider trading, and to protect the small investor.

22.   **Risks and Safeguards**. The recommendation to enhance direct and portfolio foreign investment would involve lifting certain restrictions on capital movements to facilitate the sale and purchase of Korean equities and the repatriation of dividends and profits. As equity inflows increase so will potential outflows in the form of repatriable funds. Greater capital market openness can carry two sorts of risks, the risk of macroeconomic instability and the risk of loss of control of domestic assets to foreigners. Both risks can be contained, however, in ways that would be consistent with the attraction of greater amounts of equity inflows into Korea.

23.   The risk of macroeconomic instability arises from the possibility of large and volatile capital flows. Large inflows can occur in response to high domestic interest rates and stock prices--this would tend to lead to exchange rate appreciation which, in turn, would damage export competitiveness. At other times, when the economy is sluggish or political instability prevails, large amounts of capital could flow out--this would reduce the resouces needed to pull the economy out of recession. The experience of Chile, Argentina and Uruguay during 1979-81 is often cited in support of this contention. If large inflows and outflows occur within a short period of time the costs of adjustment and readjustment to them (in terms of resource movements across sectors) might be quite large.

24.   The above-described risk of macroeconomic instability is limited in Korea's case by the fact that, unlike in the Latin case, such liberalization of capital movements as will be necessary will be occurring in a very strong macroeconomic context featuring a modest fiscal deficit, a strong current account, a relatively undistorted exchange rate, low inflation and a tradition of economic policy-making of high calibre and credibility. Thus the best way for Korea to contain the possible risk of macroeconomic instability would be to maintain the economic policy regime it has in place currently. Moreover, complete or immediate liberalization of the capital account will not be necessary to attract greater amounts of equity inflows--partial and selective liberalization should suffice. At the same time, monitoring of "large" capital movements should be continued.

25.   As far as the risk of losing control over domestic assets is concerned, several measures can be undertaken to ensure that liberalized portfolio foreign investment does not lead to management take-overs by foreigners. Several safeguard mechanisms have been experimented with in other countries, and Korea can easily adopt one or the other of such mechanisms (see paras. 3.36-3.41). It is recommended here that foreign holdings be restricted to a separate class of non-voting or restricted voting shares. Both the amount and the allocation of such investment can be adequately controlled in the context of a strategy of encouraging a greater amount of equity inflows than allowed at present.

26.   <u>External Financing in the Sixth Plan</u>. The external financing program of the Sixth Plan indicates that Government is cognizant of the need to modify Korea's existing external liability structure. Many of the deficiencies identified in this report have also been recognized in the Plan and several of the objectives listed in this report are in keeping with the goals of the Plan. Among the more notable financing goals of the Plan are the reduction of the ratio of short-term debt to total debt, the diversification among sources of funds, the increase of the share of equity inflows in total foreign capital inflows and the promotion of the domestic stock market through various pricing, technical, and institutional reforms. This report endorses the external liability management program of the Sixth Plan since this program would move Korea towards a model of financing consistent with its future needs and with prospective entry into the group of developed industrial economies, a group which on the basis of many economic fundamentals Korea is ready to join.

I. ASSESSMENT OF KOREA'S EXTERNAL LIABILITY STRUCTURE

A. Introduction

1.01   This report considers external financing choices for Korea. It assesses the structure of Korean external liabilities in the light of (a) general principles of liability management; (b) economic characteristics and programs specific to the country and its future evolution; and (c) developments in international capital markets. It also assesses, in the framework of these factors, the desirability and feasibility of various future financing options.

1.02   It should be emphasized at the outset that neither the level nor the composition of Korea's liabilities poses an immediate problem - they may invite attention but they do not provoke concern. Unlike most developing countries, Korea currently faces a most comfortable external financing environment characterized by an excess supply of funds and improvements in terms and conditions.[1] It is precisely this sort of "borrower's-market" environment that provides the latitude to negotiate desirable changes in external financing arrangements. Furthermore, recent developments in international financial markets have made some such modifications technically possible. A major theme of this report is that Korea should take advantage of current opportunities in international capital markets to develop better mechanisms to absorb and deflect future shocks that may emanate from the international economic system.

1.03   _International Financial Market Developments._ The pace and variety of innovations occurring over the last few years in international financial markets have been remarkable. The creation of new instruments which help to integrate markets has blurred the traditional role performed by the various credit, bond and equity markets. There have also been significant improvements in the marketability and, consequently, in the liquidity of funding instruments. This development, in turn, has widened the appeal of international financial markets, thereby attracting significant new sources of funding. Between 1982 and 1985 total borrowing in international capital markets increased by US$88 billion to US$267 billion.[2] This increase occurred despite a fall, during the same period, in syndicated bank lending from US$98 billion to US$42 billion. The trend reflects a shift towards dis-

---

1/   The currently favorable external financing situation has been created by the sharp drop in the price of oil, declining interest rates and an appreciating yen. Lower oil prices and interest rates have resulted in large cost savings on the import bill while the appreciating yen has facilitated Korean exports to OECD markets. As a result the current account is set to show a substantial surplus in 1986 and the demand for external finance is correspondingly lower.

2/   _Financial Market Trends_, OECD, No. 33, p.7. (The data exclude merger-related standbys and renegotiations.)

intermediation in international financial markets involving a change in emphasis in the role of banks. They are now reducing the extent of their traditional lending, placing greater emphasis on transferable or marketable instruments and facilitating disintermediation by a greater emphasis on underwriting of otherwise facilitating the flow of funds from investors to borrowers. For example, between 1982 and 1983 the share of securitized forms of financing in total borrowing in international capital markets increased from 44% to 80%. Finally, partly as a result of all of these developments, significant progress has been made towards dismantling barriers that traditionally have segregated national financial markets.

1.04   These integration, securitization, diversification and globalization processes taking place in international financial markets are creating enormous opportunities for both borrowers and investors. For those capable of accessing these markets, the opportunities now exist for the attainment of asset and liability portfolio structures which, if not ideal, should at least be a vast improvement on what could have been achieved only a few years ago. The manner in which such structures are attained is also equally important, since it can result in reduced costs for the borrower or enhanced benefits for the investor: in many instances, these costs/benefits could be quite significant. For example, in addition to the general decline in interest rates which has been taking place over the past three years, there has also been a decline in spreads on international bank loans. This is partly attributable to the competition being provided by new forms of financing in international capital markets. In addition to these declines in spreads on international syndicated credits, borrowers using other forms of financing have often achieved very attractive spreads over LIBOR (or some other reference rate). In fact, many prime quality borrowers have managed to receive sub-LIBOR spreads. Although not yet ranked as a prime quality borrower, a country like Korea, facing improved economic prospects, should be able to capitalize to a greater extent on the opportunities now available in international financial markets.

1.05   **Aspects of Korean Economy Affecting Desired Composition of Future Capital Inflows.** The pattern of external finance that is most desirable for a country depends to a great extent on existing and evolving features of the country's economy. For Korea the following features would seem to be most relevant.

(a) **Dependence upon International Trade.** Korea's trade-dependence is remarkably high - the sum of exports and imports amounted to about 76% of GNP in 1983-85. Because of a paucity of domestic resources (minerals, forests, agricultural goods, etc.) the country has to import in order to export and has made a living for the last twenty years on the value its labor force has added in the process of converting imports to exports. Korea's openness makes it extremely vulnerable to shocks originating in the international trading system. In particular, Korea is threatened by the recent increase in protectionism.

(b) **High Dependence on External Finance.** Korea is one of the largest users of external finance among developing countries. Changes in the terms and conditions at which international finance is available have a large effect on Korea's macroeconomic performance because its historical use of external finance has resulted in an outstanding debt of about $45 billion (end-1986 data) of which almost 60% is contracted on a floating rate basis.[3]

(c) <u>Underdeveloped Financial Sector</u>. The domestic financial system is underdeveloped and despite some liberalization measures in the last two years is still regulated by the authorities to a substantial degree. A high proportion of banks are in public ownership, including the three which effectively borrow on the Government's behalf and which set the benchmark terms for Korean debt.[4] The deposit money banks include some 45 foreign banks whose access to local currency is restricted and who concentrate on wholesale and foreign-currency business. Korean capital markets are also highly regulated and the Seoul stock exchange is somewhat peripheral given that the main industrial conglomerates have traditionally been reluctant to relinquish control by making public share issues.

(d) <u>Industrial and Corporate Finance Structure</u>. The manufacturing and trading sector is dominated by about 15 large conglomerates. These conglomerates operate across many industries, are generally undercapitalized and consequently very highly geared financially. The average (manufacturing sector) debt-equity ratio in Korea is about 3.6, compared to 3.2 in Japan and 1.0 in the US. The ratio for the conglomerates is even higher.

(e) <u>Changing Role of Government</u>. Since 1980/81 the Government has followed a gradual process of withdrawing from industrial investment and credit allocation decisions. It intends to continue doing so in the future with a view to creating an essentially market-run business environment. One implication of this is that the implicit guarantee of government support for failing industries will also be reduced <u>pari passu</u>, and the private sector will have to develop alternative mechanisms for handling business failures. It is very likely that these mechanisms will involve a different corporate

---

3/ This is not to say that sheer size makes Korea's debt unmanageable. Because of excellent export performance Korea has never had to reschedule debt payments. While Korea was the fourth largest debtor among developing countries in 1983, it ranked 16th in terms of its debt to export ratio and 15th in terms of its debt-servicing ratio. Dependence on external finance has been declining recently: foreign savings declined as a percentage of GNP from around 10% in 1980 to about 2% in 1985. In 1986 Korea reduced its external debt by about $1.8 billion thereby transferring domestic savings out of the country (on a net basis) for the first time in its modern economic history.

4/ These are the Korea Development Bank (KDB), Korea Exchange Bank (KEB) and the Korea Export Import Bank (KExim).

financing strategy than the high leverage strategy prevalent until now, a strategy that should spread project risks over a wide group of investors rather than concentrate them in a narrow group of banks.

(f) Changing Industrial Structure. Korea is moving into manufacturing sectors (e.g., automobiles, electronics) characterized by larger and riskier investments. In order to become established in these sectors Korean corporations will need more than a mastery of the basic production technology. They will need a financial structure that can see them through business downturns as well as fund an extensive production and marketing network. In the past, Korean corporations had easy access to the Government's vast financial resources. In the future, the changing industrial structure may have to be matched by a changing financial structure which spreads risks more effectively.

Table 1.1: SELECTED FEATURES OF KOREAN ECONOMY

	1983	1984	1985
Dependence Upon Trade (%)			
Exports G&S/GNP	37.7	38.9	37.8
Imports G&S/GNP	39.0	39.2	37.2
Trade/GNP	76.6	78.1	74.0
Debt/Exports	132.9	128.1	142.2
Dependence Upon External Finance			
External debt (US$ billion)	40.4	43.1	46.8
Debt/GDP	51.4	50.4	54.3
Debt service ratio	18.8	20.4	21.7
Foreign savings/GNP	2.9	2.3	1.9
Financial Sector Features (%)			
Financial assets/GNP	300	329	350
National savings/GNP	25.3	27.4	28.4
Public bank credit/Total credit /a	52.6	53.5	54.4
Debt to equity ratio (Manuf.)	3.6	3.4	n.a.
Stock market capitalization/GDP (%)	6.7	7.0	7.7

/a Public banks refer to all specialized banks and development institutions as defined by the Bank of Korea.

Source: Economic Statistics Yearbook, Bank of Korea.

B. Desirable Characteristics of Foreign Capital Inflow

1.06   There are no simple and universal rules regarding debt management nor is there a simple "optimal borrowing strategy" that can be widely applied. The appropriate structure of capital inflows will differ among countries and over time and is affected by a variety of internal and external factors not many of which may be subject to Government control. Nevertheless, a number of characteristics that new capital inflows might possess can be identified, which, if incorporated in the existing stock of external liabilities, would alleviate the most fundamental debt servicing problems facing very many developing countries. In order to act as a guide to debt management in Korea, it will, of course, be necessary to adapt these general characteristics to the particular circumstances of the country.

1.07   It is generally agreed that in addition to low cost the following are desirable characteristics of foreign capital inflow:

    (a) a wide dispersal of repayments over time;

    (b) a diversified currency composition;

    (c) a sharing of risk between borrowers and lenders;

    (d) a dispersal of risk of default inside the economy;

    (e) a correlation between debt service and the ability to pay;

    (f) a diversity of funding sources which promotes stability of supply.

1.08   Each of the above characteristics has a direct cost and may have potential indirect costs as well. The direct cost, of course, consists of the extra payment that will be demanded by lenders or investors to provide the appropriate characteristic. For example, longer maturities typically (but not always) require a larger spread than shorter maturities. Indirect costs are more subtle. It is possible for example that longer maturities may reduce the possibility of diversifying among lenders/investors since some of these (e.g. pension funds) are often restricted by regulation to short or medium term assets. This particular example also illustrates the possibility of conflicts among characteristics: acquiring more of one characteristic (maturity length) may require having less of another (diversification of sources). Clearly, the decision concerning which characteristics to emphasize in a country's external liability structure and how much of those characteristics to acquire will depend on their total costs measured in relation to the benefits they are expected to confer. Since these costs and benefits vary over time it is necessary also to pay attention to timing in the "purchase" of desirable characteristics.

Dispersal of Repayments over Time

1.09   That the maturity structure of capital inflows has important conse-quences for debt service is adequately illustrated by the problems caused in the early 1980s by a rapid build-up of short term borrowings. However, the finance literature has little to say on the issue of maturity, apart from the traditional adage that long-term needs should be financed long. This principle implies that for project related investments loan maturities should as far as possible match the economic life of the project.[5]

1.10   For non-project financing also there is a clear preference for longer maturities since the annual amortization component of debt service declines as the maturity of the loan increases and debt-service difficulties are more easily avoided because the payments are smaller in each period than would be the case with shorter maturities. These benefits are generally purchased at the cost of higher interest charges, given the normal-shaped yield curve. Indeed, considerable cost savings may exist at the short-end of the market. These cost savings, however, need to be carefully weighed against the risk of a sudden withdrawal of credit facilities and against the adverse implications for creditworthiness implied by heavy short-term borrowing. Moreover, while short-term borrowings should not be used for general balance-of-payments support nor for financing longer-term investment projects, an essential function of short-term debt is to finance imports. Given the normal pattern of import financing by 90 to 120 day credit, this would suggest that short-term debt should not exceed a level corresponding to three to four months imports. Semi-industrialized countries such as Korea which tend to import relatively large amounts of intermediate goods for further processing can probably justify a higher share of short-term debt in capital inflows than countries that import mainly consumption and investment goods.

Table 1.2: MATURITY RELATED FEATURES OF KOREA'S DEBT

	1979	1981	1983	1985
Short-term/Total debt	26.9	31.5	30.1	22.7
Medium-term/Total debt	2.8	3.2	4.8	4.9
Long-term/Total debt	70.3	65.3	65.1	72.4
Nontrade related short-term debt/ short-term debt	n.a.	24.5	22.1	32.3
Short-term debt in import months /a	3.2	4.7	5.6	4.1
International reserves in import months/a	3.4	3.2	3.2	3.0
International reserves/short-term debt	104.3	67.2	56.9	72.0

/a   Merchandise import.

Source: Ministry of Finance

---

[5] Economic life should be interpreted in general terms to mean a reasonable pay-back period geared to the nature of the project and likely stability of cash flow to be generated from the project.

1.11   Application to Korea. It was common to hear alarums about Korea's
maturity structure as recently as a year ago. Observers pointed to the legacy
of the rapid build-up of debt in 1979-80 in the form of a sharp increase in
the proportion of short-term debt in total debt (see Table 1.2), a steady
increase in the share of amortization in debt service payments (up from 8% in
1980 to 11% in 1984), and a "bunching" of repayments in the late 1980's (see
Table 1.3). The level of concern with Korea's maturity structure has declined
perceptibly in the last year or so primarily because of two developments:
(a) a steady reduction in the proportion of short-term debt, from a high of
34% in 1980 to under 23% in 1985; improvement is also indicated when short-
term debt is measured in terms of import months, the level of having fallen to
the equivalent of around four months of imports in 1985 and probably below
that in 1986;[6] and (b) favorable developments in terms of oil prices,
interest rates and the relative competitiveness of the won which, if sustained
in the medium term, will generate current account surpluses, reduce external
financing needs and allow Korea to ride over the amortization hump, which is
of moderate proportions to begin with, with ease. Given these considerations,
the maturity structure of Korean debt seems quite sound at the moment.
Nevertheless there is no harm in lengthening the maturity structure should it
be possible to do so at reasonable cost. Given the relatively flat yield
curve characterizing international capital markets these days and given
Korea's excellent economic fundamentals it would appear that Korea could
indeed get longer maturities at low cost on future financing arrangements.
Longer maturities would serve to keep future debt service payments lower than
they might otherwise be, a feature that would prove very useful in the event
of renewed high external financing needs.[7]

6/ This improvement mainly reflected efforts by Korea to reduce the use of
    trade credits. The maturity period allowed for trade credits was reduced
    from 180 days to 90 days and the eligibility for such credits was
    restricted to a narrower set of imports than before. Steps were also
    taken to reduce the volume of outstanding short-term swaps with foreign
    banks and to tighten the availability of foreign currency loans to fund
    equipment imports.

7/ Some concern has been expressed about the fact that many Korean bonds
    issued on international markets in recent years have five-year "put"
    options (which allow lenders to redeem the bond at the put date) attached
    which, if exercised, would reduce the average maturity of medium and
    long-term debt considerably. In this regard it is worth noting that the
    practice of attaching "puts" is widespread and Korean bonds are not an
    exception, that "puts" are not generally exercised unless the repayment
    ability of the borrower deteriorates drastically, and that removing such
    options from the bond contract could reduce the appeal of the instrument
    to many investors and thereby reduce the amount of diversification of
    funding sources.

Table 1.3: PROJECTED DEBT AMORTIZATION FOR KOREA, 1985 TO 1990

	1985	1986	1987	1988	1989	1990
Amortization /a (US$ millions)	4,192	4,700	4,470	4,710	4,770	3,930
As % of MLT debt at end-1985	11.9	13.0	12.4	13.1	13.2	10.9

/a On the basis of projected amortization on medium and long term debt
   outstanding of US$36.52 billion at end-1985.

Source: Economic Planning Board.

Currency Composition of Inflows

1.12   The literature is not at all clear as to what would represent an
optimum currency composition for capital inflows. In theory,[8] and in the
long run, the particular currency of denomination of debt should not matter
since exchange rates will vary inversely with interest rates. However, as
recent currency movements illustrate, departures from the "purchasing power
parity" theory of exchange-rate movements can be of long duration and of
unpredictable magnitude. Indeed, Morgan Guaranty (1984) shows that in a
situation in which exchange-rate movements do not fully reflect interest-rate
differentials, significant savings can be made by borrowing in low interest
currencies.

1.13   In determining the currency composition of capital inflows borrowers
typically seek to minimize the variability of their debt service obligations
and to minimize the cost of borrowing. These objectives correspond to the
hedging and the speculative components of a borrowing decision. The hedging
component aims at minimizing risk by insulating the economy from currency
volatility and changes in the terms of trade. The speculative component
reflects the borrowers' expectations of changes in exchange rates and interest
rates. In view of the markedly increased volatility of exchange rates during
the period of floating exchange rates and the great difficulty in accurately
forecasting such movements, it is argued here that the hedging motive should
predominate for developing countries. This strategy implies that variations
in the costs of financing resulting from exchange-rate changes should as far
as possible be matched by shifts in a country's income or exports and that
borrowers should be willing to pay to alleviate the risk involved.

---

[8] On the assumption that the premium or discount between forward and spot
     exchange rates reflects only nominal interest-rate differentials and that
     the forward rate is an unbiased predictor of the future rate.

1.14   A number of proposals aimed at reducing currency risk have been put forward. Kalderen (1985) and others suggest that the currency composition of debt should match a country's export income as closely as possible. As an alternative for countries with currencies tied to a basket, he proposes a correlation between debt and the basket. McDonald (1982) recommends choosing the currency composition of liabilities (net of reserves) in the light of the composition of the foreign currency returns of associated investment projects. However, recognizing that many projects will not have directly identifiable foreign exchange returns, he suggests linking the currency composition of debt to the general structure of foreign exchange earnings. Lessard and Williamson (1985) suggest that currency risk would be avoided by contracting debts in a bundle of currencies that match the destination of exports. Another strategy put forward is that of basing the currency composition of a country's debt on the pattern of its trade, that is, countries should borrow in the currencies they earn from exporting and hold their reserves in the currencies in which their imports are denominated. Finally, Morgan Guaranty (1984) recommends that developing countries should incur a portion of their debt in currencies other than the dollar in order to diversify their interest and exchange-rate risks. It is also suggested that the lack of a hedge [9] does not negate the potential benefits of diversification since borrowing a mix of currencies provides a degree of protection against commodity price fluctuations stemming from changes in the dollar's exchange-rate against other major currencies.

1.15   There is a high degree of consistency between the proposals set out above. In effect, all the studies agree in principle that the currency composition of debt should be closely related to the currency distribution of export receipts. In this way changes in the debtors' terms of trade would tend to offset, at least partially, the exchange-rate losses on debt amortization. However, the pursuit of such a policy in practice would be impracticable since it would involve borrowing in numerous relatively minor currencies which would not be available on international capital markets.[10] Moreover, the administrative cost of managing such a wide portfolio of currencies would be prohibitive. In the light of this there would appear to be considerable merit in Kalderen's approach that, where applicable, the composition of debt should match the shares of individual currencies in a currency basket; this effectively excludes the currencies of relatively minor trading partners. Indeed, an even more selective approach could be taken under which debt would be contracted only in a handful of major currencies which make up the bulk of export receipts. Such an approach would economize on debt management resources while at the same time ensuring that the debtor is adequately protected against the exchange-rate movements of the major currencies.

9/   Because, for example, foreign-exchange receipts are largely in dollars or because exports are priced in dollar terms in world markets.

10/   However, countries can use the technique of currency swaps to obtain currencies that may not be available to them directly.

1.16   <u>Application to Korea</u>. The existing currency composition of Korea's
debt would appear to be reasonably balanced in view of Korea's trade pattern. Some 80% of the debt is denominated in US dollars and some 12.5% in
Japanese yen. While the dollar composition appears heavy relative to the
geographical composition of exports (see Table 1.4) it would appear to be
reasonable relative to the currency composition of exports since the bulk of
exports to countries other than Japan are paid for in dollars. However, the
currency composition of the debt could become unbalanced as the pattern of
trade changes. For example, it is possible that the relative importance of
the US as a destination for Korean exports will decline in the future as Korea
pursues export diversification and/or if trade frictions with the US intensify. It is also possible that the dollar's role as the world's major trading
currency may decline and that of the yen and selected European currencies may
increase. These considerations would argue for greater representation of the
non-dollar OECD currencies in future borrowings. This would also be appropriate from the hedging point of view since so large a proportion of debt is
held in just one currency, the US dollar. Given Korea's macroeconomic sensitivity to its terms of trade and given the increased volatility of exchange
rates it would be desirable for Korea to adopt a more active currency management strategy for the future. This strategy should be based on the principle
that variations in the cost of debt-servicing that result from exchange rate
changes should as far as possible be offset by changes in Korea's ability to
pay as measured say by its terms of trade. It would be useful to develop a
set of correlations between Korea's terms of trade and various exchange rates
and use these expected correlations to guide the choice of currency in future
borrowing.

1.17   It is very likely that the application of this principle would
suggest a greater representation of the yen in Korea's liability basket. This
is so because the Japanese and Korean economies are similar in fundamental
respects and are affected similarly by major changes in the international
trade and finance environment. For example, an increase in the price of oil
affects both economies adversely and, ceteris paribus, should tend to worsen
their external balances and depreciate their respective currencies. Under
such circumstances a yen-heavy liability basket would provide a hedge for
Korea since the value of its liability would decline together with the
deterioration in its ability to service its debt. Similarly, a positive
external shock, such as a decline in oil prices, would tend to strengthen the
external balances and currencies of both countries. Korea would then be faced
with a higher debt-service burden (as the yen appreciates) but it would also
be in a stronger position to accommodate such a burden (as its external
balance improves).

Table 1.4: CURRENCY COMPOSITION OF MEDIUM AND LONG TERM PUBLIC DEBT

| | Debt Outstanding Disbursed (%) | |
	1983	1984
US$	79.2	80.1
Japanese Yen	12.6	12.4
DM	1.7	1.2
Others	6.5	6.3
Total	100	100
Memorandum Items:		
Geographical Trade Composition (%)		
Exports to US/Total exports	33.7	35.8
Exports to Japan/Total exports	13.9	15.7
Imports from US/Total imports	24.0	22.4
Imports from Japan/Total imports	23.8	24.9

Source: World Bank Debtor Reporting System; Economic Statistics Yearbook, Bank of Korea.

Project Risk Sharing

1.18   A major role of financial markets in industrial countries is that of assisting risk diversification and the transfer of risk from more risk averse to less risk averse agents. This aspect of external financial relations of developing countries has also received increasing attention in recent years. Although both borrower and lender would be willing to pay a premium to shift risk, it is possible that foreign lenders, either because of a greater ability to diversify a specific risk or a greater tolerance for bearing risk, may demand a smaller premium than the maximum the borrower is willing to pay. Because of this comparative advantage in bearing risk, the shifting of risk to the lender would make both the borrower and the lender better off. Large multinational companies, with extensively diversified business interests, typically possess such a comparative advantage in risk-bearing.[11]

11/ Reasons why direct foreign investment flows declined relative to bank loans despite the above-described comparative advantage of large multi-national firms to spread and bear risk are discussed in Chapter 4. An important reason was availability of loans at low (even negative) real interest rates through the 1970s as a consequence of a petrodollar deposit glut among international commercial banks.

1.19   Present developing country financing arrangements with their concentration on bank credits involve a rather limited degree of risk sharing. There is obviously no risk sharing by outside investors in the case of existing non-project financing. However, even with lending for a specific project or program, the prevalence of government guarantees ensures that the repayment of funds is not contingent on the success of the project. In effect, the only situation in which risk is shared with the lender/investor is in the event of debt repudiation by the government.[12/] The costs of such repudiation are such as to make this occurrence extremely unlikely and the loss experience of lenders in the post-World War II period confirms this.

1.20   <u>Application to Korea</u>. The classic medium for risk diversification is foreign equity participation, either direct foreign investment or portfolio investment. Korea's situation is characterized by the fact that less than 5% of outstanding external liabilities are in the form of equity investments. Indeed, there have only been two or three years since 1970 in which this proportion has been higher than 5% of annual flows. This situation can be contrasted with that of many other developing countries in whose cases the ratios of foreign investment to total capital inflows have ranged from about 13% (Mexico, Argentina, Philippines) to as high as 95% (Singapore).

1.21   An important reason for Korea to consider external financing instruments which have the property of project risk sharing is that the sectors which are likely to launch Korea into the next stage of economic and technological development (e.g. automotive equipment and sophisticated electronics) are characterized by larger and riskier investments. Given also that the government intends to adopt a less interventionist role in the future it will be important for domestic entrepreneurs to utilize financing arrangements which help shift these larger risks.[13/] Greater reliance by Korea on direct and portfolio investment would also be advantageous because it would reduce vulnerability to external disturbances and because of the impact of such investment on long-term growth prospects which may be improved by the transfer of technology and managerial skills that are generally associated with foreign direct investment. Moreover, the direct involvement of foreign firms in the Korean economy could help to reduce protectionist pressures against Korean goods in major export markets. Obstacles to be overcome include a traditional reluctance to cede control over enterprises to non-residents and the underdeveloped state of the Korean stock exchange which lends itself to somewhat erratic price movements. A strategy for increasing risk sharing would,

---

12/   While it could be argued that debt rescheduling involves some risk sharing on the part of the lender, to the extent that it merely postpones payments to some future date without modifying the underlying obligation, this is unlikely to be significant.

13/   The need to develop private sector mechanisms (such as the stock market) to deal with future business risk is also discussed in the context of a desirable future industrial policy for Korea in a recent Bank report entitled <u>Korea: Managing the Industrial Transition</u> (Report No. 6138-KO).

therefore, have to look at ways of achieving such sharing while minimizing
non-resident control and maintaining stock market stability.

Dispersal of Risk Inside Economy

1.22   Developments in world capital markets in the 1970s encouraged the
concentration of default risk inside the debtor's economy through the tying
together of risks of individual developing country loans via public guarantees
and cross default clauses. As a result the risk associated with most commercial bank loans to developing countries--even those earmarked for specific
projects--is ultimately borne by the government of the borrowing country. The
shift to publicly-guaranteed financing has resulted in greater flexibility for
borrowers and in better borrowing terms. However, it has the disadvantage
that, as lenders are generally unable to distinguish accurately the risk of
individual projects within a particular developing country, it leads to an
equalization of lending rates for different project risks, with adverse implications for project choice. Moreover, such concentration of risk in the
government can be harmful to the extent that (a) it encourages excessive risk-
taking on the part of both borrowers and lenders (the "moral hazard" problem);
(b) it involves Government too deeply in industrial investment decisions; and
(c) it places a potentially large financial burden on the government.

1.23   Application to Korea. Default risk is very heavily concentrated in
Korea. Such concentration is at two levels. First, the predominance of conglomerates in the Korean industrial structure means that a limited number of
parent companies is responsible for the debts of many individual borrowing
companies. Secondly, the bulk of public sector borrowing is contracted by
three state-owned banks (KDB, KEB and KExim) which on-lend to resident companies. Thus risk is also highly concentrated in the banking sector. On top of
this already concentrated banking and private-sector risk, lenders generally
perceive that virtually all (including private) Korean external borrowing is
effectively government guaranteed [14] and the recent experience of the Kukje
conglomerate tends to support this.[15] Not surprisingly risk concentration is
also high in the case of domestic credit. Again a few conglomerates are
heavily indebted to a few banks and, because of the past use of the banking
system as an instrument of Government industrial policy, the ultimate risk is
considered to be borne by the Government whether or not explicit guarantees

---

14/   Over 80% of total external debt is formally guaranteed by the Korean
      Government. However, the proportion of debt that is effectively
      Government guaranteed is undoubtedly higher still.

15/   The Kukje conglomerate went bankrupt in 1985. None of its foreign
      creditors were, however, adversely affected as the Government assured
      them that their loans would be repaid. The moral hazard problem has been
      particularly evident in the construction and shipping industries in which
      firms grew recklessly on the strength of credit. Despite low profit-
      ability and excessive gearing on the part of borrowers, lenders were
      willing to lend on the basis of government-guarantees which, indeed, did
      not have to be explicit in all cases.

exist. While methods of reducing this risk concentration would be beneficial to project selection, this advantage might be partly offset if it were pur- chased at the cost of higher borrowing rates for the already highly geared private sector. In the long run, however, there should be advantages to pursuing instruments that maximize risk dispersal. In general, such instru- ments include non-guaranteed corporate bonds, non-recourse finance (i.e., loans that can be serviced only out of revenues generated by the project), equity investment and various new forms of investment such as production shares or incentive contracts. Under all these alternatives the lender would have a strong interest in assuring the project is well conceived and executed, and would understand that government relief would not be forthcoming in case of project failure.

Ability to Pay Considerations

1.24   The shift in the composition of capital inflows to developing countries towards more reliance on bank credit and less on equity has resulted in a pattern of debt service payments that is unrelated to, or (as has been the case in the recent period of falling commodity prices) perversely related to ability to pay. In the case of fixed interest debt, the existence of fixed external obligations exacerbates the impact of sudden revenue shortfalls since the absolute decrease will represent a larger proportionate decrease of net revenues than of gross revenues. The experience with floating rate debt has been even more painful for developing countries: such debt allied to the record interest rates (both nominal and real) of the early 1980s greatly increased the volatility of debt service obligations by spreading increases in interest rates not only to newly contracted debt but also to all existing floating rate debt. Moreover, the coincidence of high interest rates with declines in national income of many developing countries impaired these countries' ability to maintain debt service.

1.25   A desirable characteristic of capital inflows is, therefore, that debt-service obligations should be related to the borrower's ability to pay. In particular, the problems created by a repayment pattern which is indepen- dent of unexpected changes in terms of trade and of the success or failure of particular projects have focussed attention on the need for equity type finan- cial instruments that would link repayments to outcome. The attractiveness of such instruments is borne out by a recent study of twelve developing countries (not including Korea) which concluded that total returns on foreign direct investment are more correlated with a country's ability to service its external liabilities (as measured by growth of GDP) than are interest payments on external debt (International Monetary Fund, 1985).[16]/ The greater the association between movements in service obligations and in output, the less the reduction in expenditure required to generate resources to meet service payments and, consequently the greater the contribution to the external adjustment process.

_____

16/ The IMF (1985) study also showed that the incidence of debt rescheduling was lower for countries that had a higher fraction of their external liabilities in the form of equity investments.

1.26   Too fine a point should not be placed on this role of equity
instruments in the external adjustment process because the foreign exchange
impact of such instruments arises not just from dividend remittances but also
from reinvested earnings. There is some evidence that suggests that reinvestment earnings tend to decline as domestic economic conditions deteriorate and,
if this component is large relative to the dividend remittance component, the
net impact on the external adjustment process could be similar to that of
service payments on external debt. Nevertheless the evidence also indicates
that foreign investment inflows, whether new or reinvested are strongly
affected by the host country's economic policies. A set of appropriate
exchange rate, interest rate and other macroeconomic policies is likely to
have a stronger and more durable effect on the pattern of foreign equity
investment than transient phases of the business cycle. To this extent the
importance of such investment in aiding adjustment to an external shock is
partly subject to policy control. A related matter pertains to the relative
costs of dividend payments and interest payments. Since equity investment is
riskier than lending, the average dividend rate should be higher than the
average interest rate in order to compensate the investor for accepting higher
risk. Thus, while the payments on equity instruments may tend to correspond
better to the ability to pay, it should be remembered that, on average, they
will also be higher than payments on debt instruments.[17]

1.27   Application to Korea. The size and nature of Korea's outstanding
debt (about $47 billion of which almost 60% is repayable at floating rates) is
such that macroeconomic performance is vulnerable to even small changes in
international trade and finance arrangements. Even under optimistic assump-
tions regarding the need for future inflows the annual debt service bill is
due to rise steadily and substantially from about $7-8 billion in 1985 to
$10.8 billion 1991 (see Table 1.5).[18] Given an optimistic export growth rate
projection of 11.5% during 1987-91 this debt service burden would appear to be
quite manageable. Should such export growth not be possible the task of
servicing the debt becomes daunting indeed. In view of the importance of the
external sector to Korea's economic welfare it would appear imperative for the
country to develop external financing arrangements that at least have the
potential of aiding in the process of external adjustment.

17/   The Economist (March 15, 1986, p. 67) reports that from 1978 to 1983 the
        average foreign exchange cost of servicing direct investment was less
        than 5% compared to the average interest cost of 13% on bank loans.
        While this was probably due to the extraordinarily high interest rates in
        the early 1980s this finding could also arise from high rates of rein-
        vestment brought about by high expectations of future earnings.

18/   The scenario shown in Table 1.5 is based on the optimistic schedule of
        external financing requirements that underlies the Sixth Plan. Should
        Sixth Plan assumptions for export growth and domestic savings not be
        validated by actual experience, the servicing of the debt accumulated in
        the early 1980s will exercise a considerable drag on the economy for the
        next several years.

Table 1.5: KOREA's DEBT SERVICE
(US$ million)

	1977	1979	1981	1983	1985
Historical Debt Service					
Total debt service	1,479	2,971	5,772	6,351	7,879
Interest	650	1,354	3,476	3,187	3,687
Amortization	829	1,617	2,296	3,164	4,192
Debt service ratio (%)	10.8	15.3	21.2	20.9	23.9

Projected Debt Service	**1986**	**1987**	**1988**	**1989**	**1990**	**1991**
Total debt service	7,920	8,820	9,420	10,005	10,440	10,790
Interest	3,920	4,220	4,370	4,455	4,540	4,590
Amortization	4,000	4,600	5,050	5,550	5,900	6,200
Debt service ratio (%)	20.5	20.5	19.2	18.7	17.6	16.4

Source: 1977-85, Ministry of Finance; 1986-91, Economic Planning Board.

1.28   Whether external financing in the form of direct and portfolio investment has this property in the Korean context cannot be conclusively established from available data. The data, however, do support the general presumption that repayments associated with such equity inflows tend to be more related to the ability to pay than are repayments necessitated by debt inflows. For example, simple correlations over the period 1977-85 show that while the debt service ratio has been negatively correlated with GNP growth in Korea (r = -0.32) the "investment service" burden (total remittances divided by exports) has been positively correlated (r = 0.20). The low degrees of correlation and the small sample sizes caution against forming definite con- clusions, however. Furthermore, the cost of equity inflows relative to debt has been declining since the early 1980s. Indeed, dividend payment rates have typically been less than interest rates (See Chapter 4). Also, while during the 1970s almost 75% of total annual earnings on foreign investment was repatriated and the rate of reinvestment was accordingly low, this appears to have changed in recent years as a more encouraging environment has been created for such investment. For all of the above reasons it would appear to be in Korea's interest to increase the proportion of equity inflows in future external liabilities.[19]

Assured Access to External Finance

1.29   One of the main features of the world economy since the early 1970s has been increased instability in key variables which has resulted in volatile capital flows to developing countries. An important objective for developing countries therefore is to maintain a steady flow of finance, within limits determined by creditworthiness considerations. A secure flow of external finance facilitates the planning process, permits the smooth absorption of real resources, avoids over-rapid balance-of-payments adjustment and maintains borrowers' debt servicing capacity. The most effective method for developing countries to enhance the stability of inflows is by pursuing credible economic policies over a period of years. Apart from that, within the narrower con- fines of debt management, stability would be fostered by avoiding an overcon- centration of inflows from any particular capital market or group of investors or type of instrument. An optimal mix of various types of financing would be such that changes in any one component could be absorbed by changes in another without having excessive impact on either borrowers or lenders. The recent trend in international capital markets towards shifting the financing of developing countries from the commercial banks, where it is dominated by a few key players, to securities markets, which are more atomistic and anonymous is consistent with this strategy. It could be argued that the growing integra- tion of international financial markets might undermine the effectiveness of diversifying sources of borrowing since, if there was a significant positive covariance across both lenders and instruments credit sources would dry up simultaneously when crises occur. This conclusion, however, would not hold in the presence of market rigidities and segmentation and there is indeed evi- dence that such imperfections continue to exist despite growing integration. As a result, a policy of diversification of markets and instruments is likely to increase the stability of a given capital inflow and, in certain circum- stances, may even increase the level of inflows available to the debtor.

1.30   **Application to Korea.** The "stability" characteristic of capital inflows suggests that other forms of external finance including international bonds, direct investment and portfolio investment should be substituted for

---

[19] This should not be taken to construe that bank finance cannot play a role in adjustment. The evolution of bank lending to Korea since 1970 shows heavy concentrations of net transfers around 1975-74 and 1979-82, a fact which suggests that bank finance has played a countercyclical role his- torically. However, more than half of the loans arranged during 1978-82 were short-term loans and carried extremely high interest rates. Furthermore, the repayment obligations of such finance were both large in scale and inflexible in character. Finally, the heavy borrowing of the late 70's has brought Korea close to the country lending limits of most of its traditional banks. This raises the possibility that these banks may be less accommodating to Korea in the future than they have been in the past.

bank credits; that as many capital markets as possible be tapped and, within the various markets, that a wide range of investor groups be targeted. Korean external liabilities are extremely concentrated in terms of instrument, currency and market. While the use of bond finance has increased in recent years (to about 24% of total inflows) much of this paper is subject to four or five year "put" options (which allow investors to redeem the paper at or after the put date) and is held by international banks and not passed on to non-bank investors. Thus, this type of finance is not very different from medium-term bank credits. As regards other instruments, foreign equity investment in Korean shares is confined to a limited number of investment trusts and convertible debenture issues (see Table 3.4). With regard to diversification by market, Korea is one of the few developing countries to have access to international bond markets. Although public issues have been made in the Japanese, German and Swiss markets, because of fears of an inadequate credit rating, Korea has not so far attempted to access the domestic United States or United Kingdom markets. Thus, there is considerable scope for Korea to further diversify capital inflows by market and instrument.

C. Comparison of Instruments

1.31   The previous section has discussed a number of characteristics that are generally considered to be desirable features of a country's external liability structure. The next step is to select from the large number of possible instruments and financing arrangements those that embody to the greatest extent the desirable characteristics just outlined. Since the number of possible instruments is very large it is convenient to group them into three broad categories, syndicated loans, bonds, and equity instruments. The comparison of these instruments is summarized in Table 1.6 which cross-classifies instruments by desirable inflow characteristics in the light of Korea's experience so far.

1.32   The comparison permits several broad conclusions. First, conventional syndicated loans are found to rank lowest in all the characteristics considered. Developing countries are not typically offered maturities in keeping with project duration and payback considerations, and Korea has not been an exception in this regard. Indeed there has been a shortening in the average maturity offered on new medium and long term loans in recent years. As far as debt service is concerned, Korea has never yet had to reschedule or renegotiate its obligations but this redounds to the credit of Korean economic management, and not to the flexibility of the loan instruments concerned. Indeed, the high level of servicing expected in the rest of this decade has tied Korea to the wheel of exports even more tightly. A lower than expected rate of growth of exports would significantly increase Korea's adjustment burden given its present structure of external liabilities. Macroeconomic policy is thus constrained to the extent that trade surpluses must be generated to meet debt servicing obligations. As far as diversity of funding sources is concerned a few large banks dominate the supply of international syndicated credits to Korea: the bulk of its syndications are arranged by large American and Japanese banks and participation by smaller regional banks and European banks has tended to be low.

Table 1.6: CLASSIFICATION OF INSTRUMENTS BY INFLOW CHARACTERISTICS

Desirable inflow characteristics	Instruments		
	Loans	Bonds	Equity
Long maturities	L	M	H
Diversified currencies	M	M	M
Risk sharing	L	L	H
Risk dispersal within economy	L	L	H
Correlation of debt service with ability to pay	L	L	H
Diversity of Sources	L	M	H

Code: Extent to which instruments embody desirable characteristics
       L = little, M = moderately; H = to a large extent.

1.33   A second conclusion is that bonds have only been marginally better than syndicated loans in respect of the characteristics being considered. While Korea has shifted a significant portion of its debt to bond-type instruments in recent years this has brought about only minor improvements in currency exposure, maturities, or lender diversification. Korea's access to European currencies remains limited although there have been a couple of forays into the West German and Swiss bond markets. Most Korean bonds carry eight year maturities but with a five-year put option which effectively limits the maturity to the put date. Finally, the market for Korean bonds has been limited to a rather narrow group of commercial banks, many of whom have simply substituted bonds for loans in their Korean exposures. Corporations, money funds and individual investors have not been attracted to Korean bonds in significant numbers. By and large, except for some lowering of cost (narrower spreads), Korea does not appear to have benefitted significantly from replacing conventional syndicated floating rate loans with conventional bonds and notes. The experience of other countries, however, indicates that Korea has not adequately exploited the bond markets potential for increasing maturities and diversification.

1.34   A third conclusion that follows from the comparison is that equity instruments score well on all characteristics: they do not give rise to foreign exchange risk, their maturities are linked to the life of the project being financed, debt service depends on degree of project success, risk is effectively spread among the investors, the sources of finance tend to be diversified and macroeconomic adjustment is typically made easier. A logical inference to be drawn from the above is that Korea should seek a larger proportion of future capital inflows in the form of equity investments.

1.35   In the case of Korea these general conclusions may merit some refinement. First, the classification of instruments is too broad. Instrument innovations are proceeding at a rapid pace in international capital markets and it is well known that within each of the three categories considered in Table 1.6, there now are many different instruments which vary significantly in properties. Korea may be well placed to take advantage of some of the more beneficial instruments. Second, the costs and benefits of each instrument need to be examined in the light of the actual constraints and experience of Korea and not just in theoretical or conceptual terms. In some cases, while some instruments may appear to be extremely beneficial to Korea, they may not actually be available to it. In other cases the true costs can only be determined empirically and after experience. These considerations are dealt with in the next three chapters which discuss financing options for Korea in the market for loans, notes and bonds (Chapter 2), the market for portfolio foreign investment (Chapter 3) and that for direct foreign investment (Chapter 4). For each market, recent innovations and recent developments are reviewed and the potential for Korean access is evaluated. Recommendations for future action are offered in Chapter 5.

1.36   **Risks and Safeguards:** The recommendation to enhance direct and portfolio foreign investment would involve lifting certain restrictions on capital movements to facilitate the sale and purchase of Korean equities and the repatriation of dividends and profits. As equity inflows increase so will potential outflows in the form of repatriable funds. Greater capital market openness can carry two sorts of risks, the risk of macroeconomic instability and the risk of loss of control of domestic assets to foreigners. Both risks can be contained in ways that would not be inconsistent with the attraction of greater amounts of equity inflows into Korea.

1.37   The risk of macroeconomic instability arises from the possibility of large and volatile capital flows. Large inflows can occur in response to high domestic interest rates and stock prices--this would tend to lead to exchange rate appreciation which, in turn, would damage export competitiveness. At other times, when the economy is sluggish or political instability prevails, large amounts of capital could flow out--this would reduce the resources needed to pull the economy out of recession. The experience of Chile, Argentina and Uruguay during 1979-81 could be cited in support of this contention. Whereas OECD countries with larger GNP's might be able to cope satisfactorily with volatile capital flows (of the magnitude so far experienced) Korea with its smaller GNP might be affected more severely. If large inflows and outflows occur within a short period of time the costs of adjustment and readjustment to them (in terms of resource movements across sectors) might be quite large.

1.38   The scenario just drawn, however, is unlikely to occur in Korea because, unlike the Latin countries, Korea will be liberalizing from a base situation in which no large or unsustainable macroeconomic imbalances exist: at present the fiscal deficit is modest, the current account is strong, the exchange rate is not distorted and inflation is very low. Also, the policy credibility factor which was missing in the Latin example, is strong in Korea's case and the record of the Government in managing the economy is excellent. Finally, the magnitude of the net annual inflows that might be expected from further liberalization is not so large as to provoke concern. Since Government seeks to reduce net borrowing sharply over the next few years it is likely that the bulk of the expected equity inflows will simply replace existing debt inflows. As already argued, the replacement of debt by equity inflows should aid the process of adjusting to external shocks.

1.39   Thus, the best way for Korea to contain the possible risk of macroeconomic instability would be to maintain the economic policy regime it has in place currently. At the same time, continued monitoring and control of "large" capital account transactions could be continued. Complete or immediate liberalization is not necessary to attract greater amounts of equity inflows--partial and selective opening up should suffice.

1.40   As far as the risk of losing control over domestic assets is concerned, several measures can be undertaken to ensure that liberalized port-folio foreign investment does not lead to management take-overs by foreign-ers. Several safeguard mechanisms have been experimented with in other countries and Korea can easily adopt one or the other of such mechanisms (see Chapter 3 for discussion). Both the amount and the allocation of such inflows can be adequately controlled in the context of a strategy of encouraging a greater amount of investment than allowed at present.

II. FUTURE FINANCING OPTIONS: LOANS, NOTES, BONDS AND SWAPS

2.01   This chapter examines future financing options for Korea in international loan, note and bond markets. Before future financing options are
analysed, however, it is useful to consider the factors that influence Korean
access to international capital markets. An understanding of these factors
should help in assessing the scope and limitations of Korean initiatives to
affect the supply of foreign funds.

A. Determinants of Market Access for Korea

2.02   Discussions with market participants, a review of press comments and
the literature on the determinants of market access for developing countries
suggest that the following are the most important factors influencing Korea's
market access.

2.03   Debt Size. The absolute amount of Korea's foreign debt is undoubtedly the most significant factor affecting its access to external finance.
The effects of the second oil crises, the macroeconomic policies pursued to
overcome these effects, the increase in the local won value of the US dollar
(in which the bulk of external debt is denominated) and high US interest rates
(in the context of a country relying to a large extent on floating-rate debt)
have pushed Korea's external debt to the fourth highest level for developing
countries.

2.04   Debt Concentration. The bulk of Korea's external debt is concentrated in banks. There would also seem to be a regional factor taken into
account in asset portfolio management by banks. In particular, banks
recognize regional instability factors. For example, developments in the
Philippines and the possibility of protectionism growing in the USA and the
EEC influence banks in assessing their appropriate degree of exposure to the
Asian region. Since lending to Korea tends to dominate certain banks' books
in that area and since other countries in the region have been more successful
in switching some of their funding requirements to non-banks, the movement of
some major banks' 'Asian books' to Asia may have tended to highlight the
extent of banks' exposure to Korea.

2.05   Creditworthiness Criteria. While Korea performs well in respect of
many of the economic factors influencing creditworthiness, it is clear that
some of these cause anxiety. The debt-service ratio at around 21% is high
relative to most countries in the area and is exceeded mainly by Latin-
American countries.[20] Some banks may also be placing more emphasis on the

---

20/   If short-term external debt is taken into account the position is more
      serious. While the IMF has accepted that the funding of foreign banks' A
      accounts may be treated as long term, they are cited as a negative factor
      in periodicals. The level of the guaranteed profit on these funds may
      also be in conflict with the 'spread' objective on external debt financ-
      ing. The extent of corporate external debt and the debt of overseas
      offices of Korean banks also tend to be highlighted.

ratio of net external debt to GNP. In the case of Korea, this ratio tends to be high relative to other countries in the area due to Korea's low level of foreign exchange reserves (currently about $8 billion).[21] The low level of reserves also affects the imports/reserves ratio and the reserves/GNP ratio. There are also some indications that banks take into account a country's net position with the international banking system. Korea may, therefore, be losing out from the fact that a significant portion of its reserves is not held with banks.

2.06   Political Factors. The perceived threat from the north, civil unrest and pending political changes introduce a risk factor into the Korean situation. The hosting of the Olympic games and the Presidential election in 1988 tend to highlight this issue. Developments in the Philippines may also have had a greater negative impact on lenders/investors perceptions of Korea than on other countries in the region.

2.07   Aspects of Industrialization Process. There is some concern about the overreliance on a few large conglomerates for Korea's industrialization to date. In particular, the perception is that these conglomerates are too dependent on debt financing and on the use of cross guarantees (between companies). They have an overreliance on the United States and Japan for technology and trade: inter-group trade is also quite significant. Poor accounting and audit standards and a general lack of group consolidated accounts make banks nervous about the possibility of weaknesses which are not apparent from the data available to them.

2.08   Degree of Development of Financial System. The lack of a well developed financial system, including the stock market, is a concern to lenders/investors. The private banking system is weak and presently relies on government assistance, while foreign banks are restricted in the type of business they can conduct. Public sector banking institutions are assigned a very significant role in Korea. The banking system is, therefore, perceived as not being very well developed. Similar anxiety is expressed about the 'thin' and (almost entirely) 'closed' stock exchange.

2.09   Degree of Awareness of Korean Affairs. A lack of awareness of Korean affairs and of (readily available) information about Korean developments constrains Korea's access to markets, particularly to non-bank investors. This may be partly attributable to the fact that Korean companies are engaged in a considerable amount of intermediate sales to companies: the marketing effort normally associated with (final) consumer sales would tend to have the spin-off of also promoting awareness of the country of origin of the companies marketing their products.

2.10   There is some evidence that Korea's market access, at least in Europe, may suffer from a lack of the type of traditional linkages enjoyed by

---

21/   There also appears to be some concern about the inclusion of receivables in the reserves. This also helps to explain the relatively low level of Korean funds held with foreign banks.

ex-colonial countries. For example, countries like Hong Kong, Singapore, Malaysia, and India have long historical links with Europe. Investors (particularly nonbank) in Europe lack detailed knowledge of the Korean economy and this, in itself, may make them reluctant to invest in that country. Among outsiders, Japanese banks and companies are most familiar with Korea and, as a consequence, have tended to be Korea's most prominent financiers. While American banks have historically been the chief source of external funds, there is a remarkable lack of awareness of Korea in the US capital market.

2.11   Assessment. A combination of the above-mentioned factors has produced a situation in which, despite its excellent economic performance for almost two decades now, Korea does not enjoy the best terms on its external financing among its peer countries. It has typically had to pay higher spreads and front-end fees and to settle for shorter maturities. A comparison of typical spreads with other Asian countries is presented in Table 2.1 below.

Table 2.1: TYPICAL SPREADS - SELECTED COUNTRIES, 1983-85

Singapore	1/8	Malaysia	1/8 - 1/4
Hong Kong	1/4 - 3/8	Thailand	1/4 - 3/8
China	1/4 - 3/8	Indonesia	1/2 - 5/8
		Korea	1/2 - 5/8

2.12   While Korea continues to effect a lengthening of the maturity structure of its debt, there is evidence that banks are reluctant to extend long-term facilities. The size and concentration of debt have also tended to restrict Korea's funding options and even when it has used securitized instruments, these have tended to be restricted in maturity and have usually failed to achieve the desired objective of diversifying the holders of its debt.

2.13   The foregoing also points to actions that Korea might undertake in order to improve its creditworthiness. Among such actions might be reducing the debt service ratio, increasing the proportion of reserves, diversifying away from banks by reaching out to the nonbank investor community and improving the workings of the domestic stock market. Actions along the above lines would help in providing Korea a status within the financial community commensurate with its (rapidly improving) status in the world industrial community.

B.   International Syndicated Credits

2.14   The development of the international syndicated loan was considered to be a major financial innovation in the early 1970s as it enabled enormous amounts of medium-term lending to be channelled to developing countries without seeming to place individual banks, the members of the syndicate, at great risk. Nevertheless, the recession of the early 1980s combined with unprecedented high interest rates and declining commodity prices (including that of oil) resulted in severe repayment difficulties, difficulties that have rocked both large international banks and many developing countries (e.g.

Brazil, Mexico, Argentina), thereby casting doubt on the efficacy of the international syndicated credit as a tool for development finance. Since the early 1980s, activity in the international syndicated credit market has slowed considerably (see Table 2.2) in reaction to the debt crisis while activity in competing, more liquid, instruments such as bonds and notes has increased substantially. The decline has been sharpest for developing countries as a whole--the total amount of funds raised by such countries in the form of syndicated loans fell to $9 billion in 1985 or less than 25% of the level reached in 1982. Countries in Asia now dominate this segment of the market as "voluntary" loans to the Latin America borrowers have dried up.

Table 2.2: INTERNATIONAL SYNDICATED CREDITS

	1982	1983	1984	1985
		(US$ billion)		
Borrowers				
OECD	54.8	32.0	28.7	19.3
OPEC	8.0	7.3	3.0	3.0
Other LDCs	32.5	24.9	19.8	13.1
Other	2.9	3.0	5.5	6.7
Total	98.2	67.2	57.0	42.1
LDCs excluding 'managed' loans	40.5	17.9	11.7	9.0
Of which:	n.a.			
Korea	–	3.5	3.7	3.6
Malaysia	–	1.4	1.0	0.2
Thailand	–	0.4	0.8	0.4
Indonesia	–	2.0	1.6	0.1

Source: OECD _Financial Market Trends_, various issues.

2.15   In one sense Korea has bucked this trend since it continued to have access to this market. Indeed it has been the single largest borrower from the Asian region in recent years. Nevertheless the effects of the perturbations in international financial markets are also being felt by Korea. Large US banks, which provided the bulk of syndicated credits to Korea in the past, have been reducing their exposures in relative, and in some cases, absolute terms as their global portfolio allocation strategy has responded to changes in domestic banking regulations and equity market pressures. Net lending to Korea by US banks declined from $2.3 billion in 1981 to $700 million in 1983. In 1984 and 1985 the flow was actually reversed as net lending averaged about minus $1.25 billion. The slack thus created has been largely taken up by Japanese banks and by alternative financing arrangements such as notes and bonds. The proportion of gross annual external financing arranged through loans has dropped from an average of about 89% in 1977-81 to about 57% in 1983-85 (see Table 2.3).

Table 2.3: COMPOSITION OF GROSS BORROWING (%)

	1977-81	1982	1983	1984	1985
Loans	89	86	57	59	56
Bonds	2	6	13	23	31
Other	9	8	20	18	13

Source: Ministry of Finance.

2.16   The relative disadvantages of loans as financing instruments have been detailed in Chapter 1 in the discussion of desirable characteristics of external liability structure. Some of these disadvantages were brought home forcefully to developing countries in the debt crisis that emerged in 1982. In thinking about future financial options for developing countries it is worthwhile considering some of the many innovations that have been developed or proposed for consideration within the framework of the syndicated credit market. Among these the ones most often proposed as being useful for developing countries are flexible maturity loans, graduated payment loans and shared equity loans.[22]

2.17   Korean Potential for Innovative Loans. Korea's relatively high export/GDP ratio makes it vulnerable to external shocks. Therefore, in judging the contribution of any proposed instrument to improving the structure of Korea's external liabilities, a major consideration must be the degree to which variations in export earnings would be reflected in the time profile of debt service payments. Judged by this criterion the smooth path of debt service payments made possible by a variable maturity loan would generally be welcomed: although it is not directly related to the economy's ability to pay it does at least reduce uncertainty and permit the earmarking of funds for future debt service. However, a lengthening of loan maturity would only be justified when this coincided with a deterioration in Korea's ability to pay. Thus, the postponement of amortization by way of extending loan maturities would have been appropriate for Korea in the mid-1970s. By contrast, the persistent decline in inflation and buoyant export markets since the early

---

22/ Under a flexible maturity loan arrangement debt service payments are held constant and the amortization period fluctuates to offset the effects of changes in floating interest rates. Under a graduated payment arrangement debt service payments begin below those applicable to a standard loan for the same period and increase sufficiently over time to allow the loan plus interest to be repaid by the maturity date. Shared equity loans are loans offering a share in the equity of the enterprise in return for below market rates of interest. A more detailed discussion of these arrangements is provided in the Appendix to this chapter.

1980s, means that the use of this instrument would not have been suitable or indeed necessary in this period.

2.18   One possible source of shared equity loans to Korea would be international venture capital funds which might be attracted by the opportunity to share in the impressive growth of the Korean economy. Shared equity loans would provide such investors with a means of avoiding some of the controls restricting foreign portfolio investment or permit them to participate in the fortunes of unquoted companies, while at the same time avoiding any dilution of control for the owners of the firms. Nevertheless, it must be recognized that foreign demand for such instruments would be limited to a relatively small portion of overall equity portfolios and that a concerted marketing campaign would be required to ensure a worthwhile flow of capital from this source.

2.19   Realistically speaking, it is difficult to imagine that such variations in traditional syndicated credits will be available to Korea on attractive terms. Until a large number of lenders are attracted to such instruments, it is unlikely that competitive terms will be available on any of these variations.[23] Given that many foreign (and particularly US) banks involved in lending to Korea already face binding country exposure limits, these instruments are presently unlikely to appeal to international banks. The existing features of syndicated credits, in particular 'grace' periods, multi-option facilities and (to a lesser extent) available maturities would appear to offer better, though not ideal, prospects for Korea. The cost of improving available options on a standard syndicated credit (e.g. a longer maturity) tend to better known and more competitively set than equivalent features on an entirely new instrument.

2.20   Within the syndicated credit market there would appear to be room for obtaining better terms and conditions through better coordination of the three major "semi-sovereign" borrowers (KDB, KEB and Kexim) as well as by more active marketing. These borrowers get varying terms despite the similarity of the underlying risk involved which leads to the inference that better coordination in terms of size and timing of requests may be warranted. Also, as already noted, Korea's market access, at least in Europe, may suffer from the lack of the type of traditional linkages enjoyed by ex-colonial countries such as Hong Kong, Singapore and Malaysia. This has affected the degree of diversification of Korea's loan syndications and suggests the need for a marketing effort aimed at making the larger banking community aware of Korea's economic strength and potential.

2.21   Better still Korea should attempt to make greater use of the notes and bonds markets in the future. In doing this it will be pursuing a strategy

---

[23] In 1985, three international syndicated credits for Korean entities included transferability options for the original lenders entitling them to sell all or part of their loan to other banks at a later time of their choosing. However, it is difficult to isolate any significant benefits from these options from the effects of other features of the facilities.

that is congruent with the securitization trend prevalent in international capital markets as well as consistent with the attainment of lower costs, longer maturities and greater diversification. In order to do so, however, Korea may have to employ a marketing approach that is different in several respects from its past strategy. Notes and bonds are discussed in more detail in the following two sections and market strategy aspects are picked up more formally in Chapter 5.

C. Euronote and Similar Issuance Facilities

2.22   Short-term borrowing programs have developed very rapidly in recent years and have proven very cost-effective for issuers. Most programs have been in the form of the Note Issuance Facility (NIF) or the Revolving Underwriting Facility (RUF), while Eurocommercial paper programs have developed more recently. Note Issuance facility is a generic term for a syndicated financing arrangement that guarantees an issue access to a certain amount of funds for a prescribed length of time.[24] At any time during the term of the facility, the borrower may request that a portion of the facility be a "drawn down," which results in an offering of short-term promissory notes. These negotiable instruments usually have a maturity of one, three or six months. The underwriting facility, however, typically extends from five to seven years thereby making these instruments medium term from the borrower's perspective.

2.23   A Eurocommercial paper program (ECP) differs from the NIF in two major aspects. The paper is not issued in large tranches but as and when investor demand surfaces. Similarly, the maturity is flexible. In addition, there is no back-up underwriting facility. Eurocommercial paper program, because of its flexibility in terms of timing of issuance and maturity are more favored by investors. Both NIF and ECP programs have proven to be a cheaper way to borrow compared to committed bank loans, syndicated revolving credit arrangements or traditional bond finance, especially in view of the relatively low cost of establishment of these programs. Besides their cost effectiveness and their flexibility, these short-term borrowing programs can provide exposure to a wider pool of investors and thus pave the way for long-term offerings. Corporations are now a significant presence in this market as both borrowers and lenders. The bank/nonbank base is now considered to be 50/50.

2.24   Competition has significantly reduced the costs of arranging such facilities, while the growth of more sophisticated features of facilities and placement mechanisms provide great opportunities for accessing both a wide range of markets and different options within those markets. A movement by

---

24/   The underwriting facility is designed to ensure that if the notes on offer are not purchased by investors, they will be sold to a group of underwriting banks who, for an underwriting fee, are committed to purchase the notes at a predetermined spread. Alternatively, these underwriting banks may provide funds through a separate lending arrangement. Underwriting commitments can run as long as 15 years, with the usual maturity in the five- to seven-year range.

large sophisticated borrowers to the issuance of Euronotes without underwriting facilities made it easier for a large number of new borrowers to enter
the market over the past year. A number of Asian countries have already
availed of NIF facilities, details of which are provided in Table 2.4.

Table 2.4: NIF ISSUES: SELECTED COUNTRIES

	1983		1984		1985	
	No.	Amount US$ million	No.	Amount US$ million	No.	Amount US$ million
Hongkong	1	36	4	102	15	944
India		-	1	100	6	280
Indonesia	4	850	2	125	8	437
Korea	11	356	5	307	6	235
Malaysia	1	150	2	120	1	41
Singapore		-	1	47	9	308
Thailand		-		-	3	175

Source: International Financing Review Country Index.

2.25   Korean Potential. The note market would appear to present
significant opportunities for Korea to replace existing short- to medium-term
floating rate bank loans with facilities which are very cost effective (often
sub-LIBOR), which reduce reliance on bank finance and which may be available
to private Korean names without need of a government guarantee. Korea's
experimentation with these facilities received a setback in early 1984 when
KEB's US$100 million attempted RUF was cut back to US$75 million due to
reluctance by some US banks to participate. However, the situation has since
improved with the success of KEB's $150 million NIF in late 1984 and KExim's
US$100 million NIF in 1985 (both for five years at 0.25%). A number of Korean
companies and private banks have also used such facilities.

2.26   While such facilities do not improve the maturity structure of
Korean debt, they are more cost effective and provide for the possibility of
debt diversification. This is because of the substantial presence in these
markets of corporations as opposed to banks. It is also possible to obtain
more geographical diversification through such facilities (especially within
Europe) as some European corporations may be more familiar with Korean 'names'
than are European banks.

2.27   Another market that could be profitably explored is the US
commercial paper market. Historically, Korean corporate names could only
issue in this market on the strength of letter of credit guarantees by US
banks. The recent acquisition of a credit rating will open up the short-term
finance market to Korean paper to a much greater extent than is presently the
case since there exist large numbers of investors in both the US and the

European commercial paper markets who are restricted by regulation, prospectus or custom from buying non-rated paper.[25]

2.28   Even with a rating, however, enhanced access to the US commercial paper market may require a "road show"--a presentation of the Korean case to American money managers. Once such a marketing effort is mounted it should be possible to float up to $200 million in short-term paper in the first year and build up to about $1 billion (on an outstanding basis) in a few years. The US CP market is very large (currently about $300 billion) and, if developed strategically, can become a major source of short-term finance for Korean businesses.

2.29   It is expected that Korea will need such funding in the future. The Sixth Plan calls for a rapid growth of Korean assets overseas and especially in the United States, as an element of an overall strategy of preserving market share. Already several Korean conglomerates have set up manufacturing plants abroad (e.g. Hyundai Motors in Canada, Goldstar Electronics in Alabama). The working capital requirements of these operations can be met through the US CP market. Given US credit ratings for Korean sovereign names, Korean corporate names could benefit from "piggybacking." Comprehensive disclosures are not required for CP issuance unlike the case for corporate bonds; this should make such issuance convenient for overseas subsidiaries of Korean conglomerates.

D.   International Bond Market Instruments

2.30   The increase in the amount of bond issuance is one of the most prominent current trends in international capital markets. Gross issues of international bonds have increased from $75.5 billion in 1982 to almost $168 billion in 1985. While the market continues to be dominated by OECD area countries and international development organizations, a number of developing countries, including Korea, have recently increased their access to it (see Table 2.5).[26] Within the overall securitization trend, a number of subtrends have implications for the future pattern of finance available to Korea. Among these are: (a) the resurgence of fixed interest bonds (straights) after a substantial decline in popularity following the high inflation and high interest rate experience of the late 1970s and early 1980s. With inflation under control in a number of industrial countries and interest rates declining, investors have been enticed back to the market in large numbers by high real

---

25/   Korea has recently been assigned a US credit rating by Moody's Investor Service and a credit assessment by Standard and Poor. Moody's has rated the Korea Development Bank an A2 (its sixth highest of 25 categories) and S&P has rated Korean sovereign risk as "satisfactory" (its third highest of six categories). These ratings are equal to those of some industrialized nations and were undertaken at the initiative of investor groups keen to broaden their holdings.

26/   Developing countries accounted for $6 billion (or 10% of total) of FRN issues in 1985.

yields. Lengthening maturities together with the facility to issue callable debt, which prevents issuers being locked into long-term high real borrowing costs--should future interest rates decline--are attractive to borrowers, such as Korea, who need to reduce their exposure to the effects of (possible) future periods of high nominal interest rates while at the same time reducing their dependence on short-term debt; (b) the recent easing of regulations in a number of countries (including Japan and Germany) which should improve the prospects for currency diversification in this market; (c) the increasing popularity of equity-related bond instruments such as convertible debentures and warrant issues. Issuing equity-related debt can be attractive option for certain types of corporations. In particular, it can be a cheap form of debt finance for a company with high earnings potential (a characteristic of many Korean firms at present) since issues by such companies would not result in any significant reduction in earnings per share. Also, coupons on such equity-related issues are often substantially below those applicable to comparable straight issues. Since strong equity markets tend to come in cycles, the timing of issuance of equity-related debt can be quite important.

Table 2.5: INTERNATIONAL BOND ISSUES
(US$ billion)

	1982	1983	1984	1985
OECD area	63.6	67.0	98.8	146.6
International development organizations	7.3	6.6	7.9	11.2
Other non-developing countries	0.5	0.9	1.2	2.0
Developing countries of which:	4.1	2.6	3.6	7.9
South Korea	(0.1)	(0.5)	(1.1)	(1.7)
Malaysia	(0.8)	(0.9)	(1.2)	(2.0)
Thailand	(0.1)	(0.3)	(0.3)	(0.9)
Total	75.5	77.1	111.5	167.7

Source: OECD: Financial Market Trends (33).

2.31   Korean Potential. Korea has had a mixed experience in the international bond market so far. Several aspects of its experience are particularly notable.

2.32   Firstly, in structuring its liabilities among currencies and between fixed and floating rate finance, Korea has had very few degrees of freedom. In the Eurodollar market, Korea currently only has access to floating rate finance and investment bankers do not foresee any significant change in this situation. In contrast, in the principal non-dollar markets, its access is primarily to fixed rate finance.[27]

2.33   Secondly, except in Japan, the creditworthiness of Korea has generally been perceived to be poor relative to peer group countries such as Malaysia, Spain and Portugal. This has been particularly apparent in both the FRN dollar market and the Euronote market.[28]

2.34   Thirdly, the customer base for Korean issues remains very limited and primarily restricted to Far East financial institutions. The Euro FRN and FRCD (floating rate note and certificate of deposit) market has to date been dominated on the investor side by Japanese banks. The combination of these instruments and the yen bonds issued by Korean borrowers amounts to almost 90% of their total securitized debt. Recent marketing efforts in Europe have paid dividends, however, in the form of successful issues. The Swiss and German markets appear receptive to further bond issues.

2.35   Fourthly, the large number of Korean issues and the small size of each issue has resulted in highly illiquid secondary market trading. Korea

---

27/   Lender familiarity and lender risk aversion are probably the two most important reasons why less than top tier credits, such as Korea, are able to tap the fixed rate market in some currencies but not in others. For example, Korea's excellent access to the yen bond market is explained by the fact that this market is dominated by Japanese financial institutions who have traditional financial links with Korea and are generally better informed about the country. In addition to unfamiliarity, lender risk aversion appears to explain Korea's lack of access to the US corporate bond market since this market is dominated by institutional investors (such as pension funds) who are very conservative and may even, in some cases, be restricted by regulations from high-risk investments. By contrast, markets such as the EuroDM market, are dominated by investors who appear to be less risk-averse and less restrained by regulations. Access to the Yankee bond market has hitherto been restricted by the lack of a credit rating for Korean sovereign or corporate risk but it is widely believed that, even with a credit rating commensurate with its present economic and political circumstances, Korea would not be be able to float Yankee bonds at terms as attractive as those available to it in the Euromarkets.

28/   An econometric study by Kyle (1985) indicates that spreads on Korean bonds have far exceeded the levels that can be explained by the various macroeconomic and international liquidity variables typically used as indicators of creditworthiness. Why Korea's perceived creditworthiness has been poorer than is warranted by generally accepted indicators is an issue that goes beyond the scope of this report. A factor that seems to be prominent in discussions about Korea relates to political risks. In addition it should be stressed that credit evaluation in the Eurobond market is somewhat primitive. There is no official rating service that provides systematic analysis.

has pursued a strategy of coming to the market frequently under a variety of names, principally, KDB, KEB and KExim--in relatively small sizes. For example, in 1985 in the Eurodollar FRN market, the average size of issue by KDB, KEB and KExim was $100 million compared to Malaysian issues that averaged $600 million. Korean borrowers, both public and private, came to the market ten times in 1985 compared to two issues by Malaysia.

2.36   Dealers in the secondary market need to maintain inventories of each issue in order to effectively make markets in these issues. There are, however, considerable economies of scale in the holding of inventories, which tend to raise the costs of secondary market trading in small issues and thus impair liquidity. This in turn implies that Korean issues typically have to carry a yield premium to compensate for the lack of liquidity.

2.37   Bonds versus Loans. Korea's historical experience in the Eurobond market has not been very successful especially when viewed from the perspective of maturities and diversification and when compared to the experience of such countries as Malaysia and Thailand. Nevertheless this market holds considerable promise provided it is approached strategically with clear long term goals in mind rather than opportunistically with a view to making the cheapest short-term deals. Floating rate notes, in particular, warrant further attention because they are superior to syndicated credits, Korea's most heavily used instrument, in terms of cost, maturity and diversity of investor base. Furthermore, while the recent acquisition of US credit ratings is expected to help Korea principally in the short-term finance markets, favorable spillover effects are also likely in the Eurobond markets.

2.38   The cost of syndicated credits is likely to remain above that of floating rate notes (of the same effective maturity) for several reasons in addition to the obvious one deriving from the lack of marketability (or liquidity) of most loans. Higher capital-asset ratios have been mandated for commercial banks by regulatory bodies (e.g. in the US) in the wake of the Latin debt crisis. As each unit of existing capital now supports fewer assets the per unit cost of maintaining risk assets has been going up. Furthermore, as banks have themselves gone to the capital markets to increase their capital they have found that they often cannot borrow as cheaply as some of their best customers. At the same time, deregulation continues to increase the competition for deposits and to bid up the deposit interest rate, thereby increasing the cost of the historically most significant source of funds for commercial banks. While interest rate deregulation may have run its course in the US, it has just began in Japan and ought to increase the cost of funds of Japanese commercial banks over the foreseeable future. Non-banks such as investment and securities firms have not experienced, nor do they face, a similar increase in cost of funds.

2.39   The potential liquidity of notes and bonds, in addition to reducing their cost to the issuer, also enables longer maturities to be established since a wider group of investors, and not just banks, are potential buyers. Thus, while it is unlikely that Korea will be able to obtain syndicated credits with maturities of more than 10 years, it would be possible for it to build up to maturities of 15-25 years in FRN's as for example has been done by Malaysia and Thailand. Indeed, Korea has already begun moving in this direction in the FRN market: four US$100 million FRN public issues were done in 1985 with effective maturities of between 10 and 15 years at the cost of an extra one-eighth of a percentage point in spreads.[29]

2.40 The wider investor base of the debt securities market offers the potential for diversification among sources of funds. How this potential is exploited depends on the marketing strategy of the issuer. To date Korea has not been very successful in reaching out to non-bank investors. However, over time, such access can be established provided a long term strategy is developed involving decisions on spreads, issuer name, a formal credit rating, marketing and choice of lead managers. Individual elements of such a strategy are discussed in Chapter 5.

2.41 <u>Application to Korea of Innovative Bonds</u>. The debt crisis of the early 1980s has highlighted the problems of volatile debt service payments and of the lack of correlation of such payments with borrowers ability to pay at different times. Among the instruments proposed to deal with these problems are index-linked bonds, constant debt service bonds and trade bonds.

2.42 In the case of the index-linked bond the principal would be regularly revised in accordance with some price index, while the interest rate would move with inflation so as to yield a fixed real rate thereby achieving a smoothening of the debt service profile. An alternative version would forecast inflation rates over the maturity of a floating rate note and then apply this forecast to both principal and interest in such a way as to ensure constant real debt service payments over time. (See Appendix for details).

2.43 A common feature of both instruments is that they would probably be more appropriate to general obligation finance than to project finance and hence would have poor risk-sharing and default-spreading characteristics. Judged from the borrower's perspective, however, the index linked bond might be preferred to the FRN. Although both instruments may have roughly equal smoothing characteristics, the index-linked bond would tend to be preferred from the point of view of diversifying sources away from banking markets and towards groups of investors less exposed to Korean paper. Thus the development of index-linked bonds could broaden the sources of capital available to Korea. Moreover, by issuing index bonds in several currencies Korea would be able to obtain a liability structure more suited to hedging its interest and currency exposure. A bond may also be available in somewhat longer maturities than an FRN.

2.44 Neither the index-linked bond nor the constant debt payment FRNs have been used in the international capital markets. Investors are generally

---

29/ As in the case of syndicated credits, after allowing for maturity differences, there appeared to be some variation between the terms achieved by the three public banking institutions, with KExim obtaining the finer terms. Surprisingly the remaining 'public' issue was by one of the conglomerates and the terms it achieved appear to be more favorable than those obtained by two of the public banking institutions.

conservative and prefer instrument innovations to be used initially for prime borrowers. Thus, from the supply side, there may be a lack of acceptance and in the case of Korea this may be equally strong in the FRN market (because of the high level of Korean paper in existing bond portfolios) and in the bank market where the inability to achieve a prime rating may raise doubts about the success of an issue. An additional disadvantage of FRNs is that banks would not be attracted to these instruments since with liabilities that are short-term and nominal there could be a maturity and interest-rate mismatch if claims were longer-term and real.

2.45   The appropriateness of instruments that smooth real debt payments depends to a large extent on the external events that accompany changes in the rate of inflation. If inflation is associated with a commodity boom, Korea as a major commodity importer, would benefit from using these instruments. However, if export markets generally are expanding rapidly it would not be desirable to postpone interest payments in this way. In the current period of declining and less volatile inflation the need for this type of instrument is, in any event, somewhat less urgent.

2.46   Borrowing via a trade-linked bond would have obvious attractions for Korea given its vulnerability to fluctuations in export markets. A trade bond, by linking payments to rates of export growth, would embody many of the desirable characteristics of capital inflows outlined in Chapter 1: debt service on such a bond would obviously be related to ability to pay, the bond would probably be issued at the longer end of the maturity spectrum, would tap new markets thereby facilitating future flows of funds, and would result in significant risk sharing between debtor and creditor. A trade linked bond, however, would undoubtedly require a government guarantee and hence would not spread the risk of default within the economy. The major difficulties with such a bond are that of attracting a significant body of investor support and of overcoming certain technical hurdles. Given the existing overhang of Korean debt in bank portfolios, the investors in such a bond would have to come from non-bank sources, and more particularly from institutional investors who require a diversified equity portfolio. With an average increase in the value of Korean exports of 12.5% between 1980 and 1984, Korean trade-linked bonds would be expected to offer a high return. Indeed, there is a risk that rapid export expansion would lead to the payment of larger amounts than would have been due under conventional syndicated loans. In view of Korea's large external commitments this may be a risk worth running. Moreover, if the bonds proved popular it would be possible to modify the relationship between exports and bond yield for subsequent bond issues.

E.   The Swap Market

2.47   In addition to accessing different markets and indeed different segments of those markets in order to achieve a desired portfolio, it is also possible to adjust the composition of asset and liability portfolios by engaging in swaps. Indeed, through the use of swaps it is usually possible to obtain certain desired characteristics of a portfolio in a more cost effective way than by accessing those market segments directly. The basic swap structures available currently allow for trades across interest rates, currencies and combinations of both (see Table 2.6).

2.48   The availability of these various swap techniques to borrowers and investors in international financial markets has significant implications for external asset and liability management. It means that it is now possible for the theory of comparative advantage to be applied to a significant extent to international financial markets. Its application to such markets would imply that borrowers should maximize their borrowing in those markets where they have a comparative advantage in raising funds, irrespective of the suitability of such funding for their own particular needs, as long as such funding can be swapped, in a cost-effective manner,[30]/ to enable the borrower to achieve an optimum funding structure. Of course, whereas it is possible to specialize completely in producing a particular good, a borrower's "comparative advantage" in any particular market (or niche thereof) may be lost if 'over borrowing' occurs. However, subject to such constraints, and the availability of suitable swaps, significant opportunities would now appear to be developing for quite sophisticated asset and liability management for participants in international financial markets.

2.49   Currently, the swap market offers the greatest depth and opportunity for restructuring existing debt, by moving into another currency or from floating rate to fixed rate debt. It is also a vehicle for reducing the cost of new borrowings. It enables borrowers to gain access to certain financial markets often at a lower cost than borrowing directly and to avoid saturation in traditional markets. In just five years, the swap market has swelled to an estimated volume of $200 billion: about $180 billion involving interest rate swaps and $24 billion involving currency swaps. It is not an esoteric or transitory market, but as demonstrated by the volume of transactions, rather it is considered by users (corporations, banks and sovereigns) as simply one of numerous funding mechanisms.

30/ Including taking account of the additional risks involved in the use of
     any particular swap mechanism.

Table 2.6: BASIC SWAP STRUCTURES

Interest Rate Swap

This involves the conversion of an underlying fixed-rate asset/liability into a floating-rate asset/liability or vice versa. It facilitates arbitraging and can also enable a borrower to obtain the desired effects of accessing a particular (fixed or floating-rate) market, or segment thereof, which, for reasons such as excessive use, lack of name within that market or inadequate credit quality, could not be accessed directly. It allows interest-rate costs and exposure to be managed without affecting the underlying source of funds. The US dollar is the most significant currency involved in such swaps, while underlying instruments include CDs, Eurobonds, etc.

Fixed Rate Currency Swap

This involves the transformation of a fixed-rate debt raised in one currency into a fully-hedged fixed rate debt in another currency. It facilitates arbitraging and allows borrowers to access markets which might not otherwise be available in a cost-effective way. Borrowers may also be able to obtain longer maturities than might otherwise be available to them if they had opted instead for direct access to a given market.

Cross-Currency Interest Rate Swap

This involves the same basic exchanges as in the fixed rate currency swap with, however, fixed rate interest in one currency swapped for floating rate interest in another currency. The main motivating influence behind this swap is the willingness of major funders, especially banks and sovereigns, to access markets for particular instruments for which they have no natural requirements, but which the swap market can use, in order to reduce costs of gaining (greater) access to a particular required currency. This swap mechanism is also used simply to restructure, or 'hedge' exposures, in existing portfolios. US dollar instruments are swapped mainly against SF, yen, DM, ECU and, to a limited extent, sterling and the Canadian dollar, while other swaps include yen/SF, yen/ECU, DM/SF, etc.

Basis Swap

This is the same as an interest-rate swap with the exception that floating-rate interest calculated on one basis is exchanged for floating-rate interest on a different basis. The basis-rate swap market may involve swapping bases such as a US dollar prime for a LIBOR, a 1-month US dollar LIBOR for a 6-month US dollar LIBOR, a US dollar LIBOR for a US dollar commercial paper, etc. It permits arbitraging spreads between different floating rate funding sources and for nonUS entities it is a way of obtaining a US commercial paper funding basis without the necessity (or expense) of complying with the stringent US requirements for a commercial paper program.

2.50   The liquidity of the swap market in general has been greatly enhanced by the fact that swaps have become traded instruments in their own right. The major commercial banks, employing their substantial capital base, now offer immediate execution as counterparties. In other words, they have started running "swap books", entering into swaps even without intermediate counterparties. Investment banks, originally only arrangers of deals, have now also established swap books, although much smaller in size. These banks now make a market in swaps which means swaps are no longer dependent on new Eurobond issues or paticular counterparty matches.

2.51   Korean Potential. Korea's lack of a credit rating and of substantial numbers of non-bank foreign investors limit its potential use of swaps. Nevertheless, the market is so deep that there should be opportunities for the country to restructure its debt advantageously, gain access to preferred markets and reduce the cost of new borrowings. A considerable part of Korea's debt is at floating interest rates; the country has limited access to bond markets which offer fixed rate funds. It could use the swap market to move some of its floating rate debt to fixed rate, locking in low interest fixed rate debt which may be available at the present time. It may also want to lock in gains from low interest debt in one currency by switching into another currency, particularly if there is fear of currency appreciation. For example, Korea currently has very good access to the yen market at competitive rates, but may prefer liabilities in other currencies. It could transform some of its low interest yen liabilities into, say, fixed rate dollars, taking advantage of its preferred access in the yen market to achieve advantageous dollar borrowings. The fact that Korea has very low coupon yen may put it in a good bargaining position with respect to sharing basis point differentials. The country may also want to diversify its liability portfolio to include borrowings in currencies other than dollars or yen. The swap market may provide opportunities.[31]

2.52   About 85% of swap transactions are conducted with a commercial bank in the middle as an intermediary between the two counterparties, absorbing the credit risk (for a fee) on both sides of the transaction. Bank intermediation has been central to the rapid evolution of the swap market by providing liquidity. A number of these banks have also played an important role as principals in the market, as mentioned above, through inventorying various swap positions and laying them off over time as opportunities arise, thereby further enhancing the depth and liquidity of the market. This means that swaps do involve further taking up available credit lines of banks. Hence, Korean access to the swap market may be limited to the extent that banks are unwilling to increase their exposure to Korea. The risk exposure is not

---

[31]/   Before entering the swap market, it is important to develop a strategy with respect to debt management, whether it is one of matching liabilities with trade flows and expected exchange rate movements of trade partners or achieving a more diversified liability structure in terms of currencies, maturities, and sources of funds. Obviously all of these goals will have to be evaluated in terms of the cost associated with the necessary swaps.

calculated on the full asset, however, thus making it more attractive than straight debt to a lending institution (or investment banks). Moreover, to date, swap exposure is not considered for purposes of reserve requirements on risk assets.[32/] However, this situation may change: the accounting treatment of swaps is coming under aggressive scrutiny by several central banks.

2.53   Changes are also occurring with respect to management of swap credit risk. For example, the World Bank has recently announced a swap insurance arrangement whereby a major insurance company provides the Bank with a line of insurance in respect of individual swap counterparties, with variable usage and pricing, depending on the magnitude of credit exposure at a given point in time. Hence, the World Bank will no longer need to use triple-A intermediary banks to undertake swaps. The swap insurance will enable it to enter swaps directly with other parties, whose credit rating may not be as strong. This presents an opportunity for Korea since it does not as yet have a triple A rating.[33/]

2.54   In sum, the swap market continues to be dynamic and growing and, as seen in the case of credit risk management, is also maturing. It is, therefore, a market that Korea, as a strong industrializing country, should now be entering. By being a sensible user of the swap market, Korea would demonstrate its own sophistication as a borrower and as a market participant concerned with liability management and least cost funding opportunities. Both KDB and KEB have undertaken a number of swaps in recent years but it is clear that as yet utilization lags behind potential. This is due partly to the lack of expertise and partly to the fact that current foreign exchange regulations constrain innovations in this area.

32/   At the time of a swap contract, the present value of the cash flows exchanged (interest and, in the case of currency swaps, principal payments) are equal. Over time, the value of the two counterparties' cash flows will change because of exchange rate and/or interest rate movements. If one party defaults, the other party assumes its original debt obligation; it may then face higher costs or a potential profit, depending on which direction currency and interest rates have moved. Thus the credit risk is the potential adverse exposure at the time of default (i.e., any positive difference between the new present value of one's remaining original debt obligation and that of the swap obligation). The range of potential risk is considered to be 30-40% of the par value of the swap, depending on the type of swap (interest rate swaps are less risky because they involve only the exchange of interest payments).

33/   It is anticipated that, over time, numerous insurance companies will enter the swap field, perhaps by forming syndicates to distribute the risk. This should enable many swap counterparties to set up multiple insurance facilities. In the future, it may be possible to utilize insurance companies in various regions of the world to provide coverage for potential counterparties in their own geographical areas. These trends may eventually enable developing countries to obtain swap insurance rather than using bank intermediaries.

SELECTED INNOVATIVE INSTRUMENTS

A. Innovative Loan Instruments

1.   A transferable loan instrument (TLI) entitles an original participating bank to sell all or part of its loan asset in the secondary market.
The borrower retains the flexibility of the syndicated loan agreement, while
facilitating participation by a larger number of banks. The large banks are
attracted to the syndicate because of the options available for offloading
part of their commitments, while other banks are attracted by the varying
maturities and denominations available under TLIs. Such instruments should be
more cost effective for borrowers. While, at first sight, the instrument
appears to introduce much-needed flexibility into the syndicated loan market,
it has a number of drawbacks. In effect, it is simply a device that recog-
nizes and brings into the open the practice of silent sub-participations which
has been taking place for some time among banks. Under such an arrangement a
bank overexposed to a particular borrower arranges for another bank to 'participate' in its loan commitment. In effect, the second gives an indemnity to
the first bank regarding part of its exposure. This device, since it is a
secret arrangement between banks, avoids the adverse effects on a borrower
from a lender attempting to offload in public part of its exposure to that
borrower. The TLI on the other hand brings such a practice into the open. If
the creditworthiness of the borrower deteriorates, the marketability of the
TLIs would not ensure its sale at close to par value. Under such circumstances the restriction of the market to banks (a common feature of TLIs)
could result in a more serious undermining of the borrower's creditworthiness
than would be likely to result from a capital market instrument under similar
circumstances.

2.   The flexible maturity loan keeps debt service payments constant by
allowing the size of the amortization payments to vary to offset changes in
interest rates. A rise in interest rates implies a fall in amortization and
hence an automatic extension of the maturity of the loan. This type of
instrument would bring considerable benefits to the borrower. To the extent
that interest-rate variations are random rather than procyclical, the variable
maturity proposal would increase the debtor's ability to pay by smoothing
debt-service payments. (If interest-rate movements are counter cyclical, as
in 1981-82, benefits would be even greater). Moreover, in terms of the
desirable inflow characteristics, loan maturities would be automatically
increased and, given their indefinite maturity, which would be unsuitable for
banks, such loans would tend to attract a new type of investor to the developing country market.

3.   Under a graduated payment arrangement debt service payments are
initially below those applicable to a standard loan for the same period and
increase over time. The graduated payment loan would also possess most of the

benefits (from the borrower's perspective) of the variable maturity loan.[1]
In addition, by relating debt-service payments to the expected profile of
project earnings, ability to pay would be considerably enhanced and, depending
on the particular arrangements in the event of actual earnings differing from
projected earnings, graduated payment loans would have the further advantage
of sharing project risk with the lender. The ability-to-pay and project-risk
sharing characteristics of capital inflows are embodied to an even greater
extent in the shared-equity instruments in which an equity share is offered in
return for below-market rates of interest. Moreover, all three instruments -
variable maturity, graduated payment and shared equity loans - being project-
type financing, would increase risk dispersal within the borrower's economy as
compared with general obligation finance.

4.   The major difficulty with these instruments is that, from the
investors' point of view, they appear to be going against the recent securitization trend in bank assets. The desire for greater asset liquidity has been
one of the factors leading to securitization, that is, the tendency to
increase the marketability of bank assets which traditionally had been held to
maturity. The risk sharing element inherent in both graduated payment and
shared equity loans together with the fact that the latter instrument would
probably require lender involvement in project management (Saini, 1985),
suggests that these two types of instrument would not be attractive to
banks. Similarly, variable maturity loans would offend against the desire of
banks for greater liquidity. Looking to other segments of the international
capital market, however, it is possible that variable maturity loans could
appeal to some long-term institutional investors for whom uncertainty regarding maturity dates is less important. Moreover, with regard to shared equity
loans, these could be attractive to equity funds as a means of participating
in enterprises whose shares would not otherwise be available (because, for
example, they are not publicly quoted or because foreign holdings are restricted). It would be unrealistic to expect, however, that a significant volume
of funds would become available from these sources. While flexible maturity
loans have been a feature of certain mortgage markets, they have not, to date,
become a feature of the international syndicated loan market.

B. Innovative Bond Instruments

Instruments that Smooth Real Debt Payments

5.   This is a particular response to the problem of volatile debt service obligations. The smoothing of real debt payments, while not being as
favorable to the borrower as mechanisms that relate payments to capacity to
pay, does at least facilitate the planning of future debt service obligations
and permits the earmarking of resources to meet these obligations.

---

[1] The exception being the automatic lengthening of maturity, although this
feature could also possibly be combined with the graduated payment loan
(see Saini, 1985).

6.   There are two basic methods of smoothing real debt payments. Williamson (1981) outlines a scheme whereby this can be achieved by issuing <u>index-linked bonds</u>. Under this arrangement the principal would be regularly revised in accordance with some price index, while the interest rate would move with inflation so as to yield a fixed real rate. To the borrower index linked bonds would have the advantage of significantly reducing uncertainty on a major item in the balance of payments by fixing the real value of debt servicing obligations. The appeal of index-linked bonds to lenders is more difficult to ascertain. It is felt, however, that some institutional investors would be attracted by the prospect of maintaining the real value of assets. The major problem with index-linked bonds, of course, is the choice of index. The use of an export price index computed for the borrowing country would be unlikely to appeal to investors. In practice it would be necessary to use a price index of the capital market in which the bond was issued. By issuing index-linked bonds in several currencies or by using a composite currency such as the SDR or ECU a borrower could obtain a liability structure that helped offset its trade or other financial exposure (Lessard, 1985).

7.   An alternative to index-linked bonds involves issuing floating rate notes (FRNs) with <u>constant real debt service attributes</u> (Goodman, 1982). This is an attempt to reconcile the preferences of many investors for stable receipts in nominal terms with the desire of borrowers to achieve smooth real debt service flows. This instrument makes use of two separate rates, a debiting factor, which is the interest charge on the outstanding balance, and a payments factor, which is the amount that the borrower has to pay each period. The debiting factor would vary with market interest rates while the payments factor would be chosen with a view to yielding equal real payments over the life of the contract. This involves forecasting future real rates over the maturity of the loan. Errors in forcasting the future real interest rate would tend to cancel out over the life of the loan since a too high forecast would accelerate payments and this would reduce the outstanding principal and hence future repayments. If inflation were high in the early years of the loan the payment factor could be less than the debiting factor with the result that amortization would be negative and the outstanding principal would increase.

8.   Both index-linked bonds and constant debt payment FRNs avoid the cash flow squeeze that can arise during inflationary periods as interest costs rise immediately while the corresponding gain in the erosion of principal only becomes relevant at the time of amortization. However, the borrower's position may not always be improved by the use of such instruments. For example, if periods of high inflation are associated with rapid growth in commodity prices and exports (as occurred in the mid-1970s) loan indexation could have the perverse effect of postponing interest payments from a period when foreign exchange was readily available to a later period when exports are stagnant. On the other hand, if rising inflation is accompanied by recession (as occurred in the early 1980s) the delay of the inflation premium in interest rates until amortization would considerably enhance ability to pay. Thus, the appropriate use of these instruments would require a knowledge of the covariances between inflation, interest rates and export receipts. Moreover, relationships between these variables would undoubtedly change over time with the result that the instruments may be appropriate when issued but may have adverse effects on ability to pay during the life of the bonds.

Trade and Commodity Bonds

9.   As an alternative to risk diversification through equity participation and direct investment much interest has been shown in the possibility of using commodity bonds. Lessard (1977) suggests that commodity bonds would be more successful than foreign direct investment in balancing the relative requirements of creditors and debtors. Interest or amortization or both on a commodity-bond would vary with the price of a commodity or basket of commodities. An essential requirement is that the price of the commodity would be precisely determined in a market largely free from price manipulation. The major attraction is that the developing countries issuing such bonds would be able to hedge the return on the bonds to the market price of its main commodity. From the investors' perspective, commodity bonds could be used either as a vehicle for speculation in commodity markets or for hedging reasons by commodity users whose income might vary inversely with a particular commodity price. The expected yield on commodity bonds would have to be higher than that on conventional bonds to compensate the purchaser for accepting a more uncertain payment stream.

10.   While Korea, not being a primary producer, is unlikely to issue commodity bonds, it may well have an interest in a close relation, the trade-linked bond. These bonds would offer a return linked to the value of a country's exports. The principal advantage for the borrowers is that trade linked bonds would permit a uniquely close correspondence between debt service payments and export revenues, thereby significantly reducing the debtor's vulnerability to external disturbances. It might also increase pressure in industrial countries against protectionism since this would directly affect the returns to bond holders resident in these countries.

11.   The disadvantages of the trade linked bond relate partly to difficulties with the definition and computation of the value of the exports of the issuing country. Decisions would have to be taken on whether to include exports of services and factor income as well as merchandise trade. The collection of data on non-trade items is notoriously difficult even in industrial countries. Another major difficulty concerns the problem of transfer pricing. Variations in tax rates in different countries enable multinational corporations to price intra-company trade so as to minimize overall liability to taxation. The scope for such practices is particularly large where a country's exports contains a large proportion of intermediate products. Thus, the value of a trade-lined bond could be quite sensitive to changes in corporate taxes among countries and to the pricing policies of multinational corporations. Such factors might undermine some investors' confidence in a trade-linked bond although it should be said that other statistical measures used in bond financing (e.g., various price indices) also suffer from measurement difficulties. The problem of moral hazard might also be considered in this context. A large proportion of trade linked debt in total liabilities might reduce a debtor's incentive to engage in export promotion or, more

likely, to reduce resources devoted to ensuring a comprehensive statistical coverage of exports.[2]

12.   Another major imponderable is the market for trade linked paper. Such paper has none of the attractions of commodity linked bonds for either hedging or speculative purposes. Trade related bonds represent a form of speculation on a debtor's future export revenues and, when exports are well diversified over the range of industry represented in a country, could be viewed as an investment in the performance of the economy as a whole. As such it could be regarded as an alternative to some of the equity funds of Mexican, Korean, Indian and Brazilian shares which have been organized in recent years. Given that investment in these funds is not without difficulties (related to thin domestic stock markets and less than rigorous accounting standards) trade linked bonds could have attractions. If this motive for holding these bonds proves to be realistic, the investment institutions would constitute the main market for trade-linked bonds, rather than the banking sector.

C. Non-Recourse Financing

13.   This type of finance aims at increasing effective risk diversification between debtor and creditor by linking borrowings to particular enterprises or projects without a Government guarantee. Since the return to the lender is dependent on the success of the project, this instrument would provide effective risk transfer. In contrast with equity or quasi-equity instruments, providers of non-recourse finance would not share a project's upside potential. The lender will require to be compensated with a higher expected return for the greater risk inherent in non-recourse financing.

14.   The attraction of non-recourse finance is that the failure of a project will not result in a loss to the government in the form of honoring guarantees to foreign creditors. There may also be other benefits since, when lending on a stand-alone basis, financial institutions have a direct interest in ensuring adequate project appraisal. Under this form of financing governments have to make it clear that they will not be liable for debts in the event of a project's failure. However, even in these circumstances, where there is doubt about the effect of a project default on a country's general creditworthiness, governments frequently assume the debts of private creditors.

15.   The combination of a largely publicly-owned banking system and the concentration of much manufacturing and trading activity in a few large conglomerates means that effective risk dispersal is extremely low in Korea. This was confirmed when one of the conglomerates failed in 1985 and the

---

[2]   A considerable amount of work would be necessary before a decision on the feasibility of a trade bond could be taken. The areas to be considered include the definitional questions mentioned above, the manner in which export returns would be reflected in bond yields and the appeal to particular categories of investors.

government compensated all foreign creditors. The international markets regard all Korean liabilities, whether contracted by the private or public sectors, as effectively government guaranteed. In these circumstances greater use of non-recourse financing would bring benefits in the areas of risk sharing and spreading default risk within Korea. However, these advantages must be set against higher expected costs of servicing non-recourse lending. Moreover, given the large gross financing requirements over the remainder of the 1980s which render Korea extremely vulnerable to market sentiment, it would obviously be necessary to move cautiously in reducing the proportion of Government guaranteed debt in total debt.

D. Interest Rate Caps

16.   Another promising instrument which has developed over the past three years is the interest rate cap. In effect, capped FRNs are a stream of interest rate options, stretching out to longer maturities than are traded on exchanges and are available in currencies such as Deutshemarks for which there are no exchange-traded interest rate options. Interest caps allow borrowers, for an upfront fee, to lock in the maximum interest rate paid. If the rate goes beyond the maximum, the cap seller pays the differential. There is considerable potential for this market, depending on the future yield curve expected. Right now the market for three to five year caps is deep and deepening further. But there are maturities going out to nine years. Interest caps tend to be in the 12%-12.5% range. Also, caps are often stripped from one security and sold to another borrower. An estimated $8 billion worth of capped floating rate instruments have been sold. Another $8-10 billion have been sold by banks. Citicorp and Salomon Brothers are the biggest market makers; they hedge themselves against the risks of the instrument by using other security markets. The users of caps are borrowers requiring protection against floating rate loans. American thrifts are buying them to cap funding costs for their portfolios of capped mortgages.

17.   There are three drawbacks to caps. First, the upfront fee can be substantial, say $1-4 million on $100 million of principal for a three to four year cap, depending on the strike level. It can go up to 5% of the principal depending on the maturity. However, as competition increases and more institutions find ways to hedge the risks, these costs may decline.[3] Second, the protection this option offers is always a second-best strategy. By its nature, it is never the most advantageous approach. But it protects against a worst case situation. Third, the present flattening yield curve makes the use of caps seem more risky than simply doing nothing -- though expectations for the future may be different. The interest rate cap market is a market worth watching however, and holds potential for developing countries, holders of considerable floating rate debt, to limit future interest obligations to manageable levels.

3/   One way of minimizing the cost of a cap is to enter into a "collar", which creates an interest rate floor as well as ceiling, for example creating a range of 8-12% for a five year maturity. Collars are usually 30% cheaper than an equivalent cap.

III. **FUTURE FINANCING OPTIONS: PORTFOLIO FOREIGN INVESTMENT**

3.01   Equity financing can be of two sorts, direct foreign investment (DFI) and portfolio foreign investment (PFI). The essential distinction between these is that the former involves the provision by the foreign investor of a package comprising capital, technology and management whereas the latter typically involves only the provision of capital. Since the costs and benefits (to the host country) of these two types of equity inflows are different and since their institutional and policy determinants are also different, they are treated separately in this report. This chapter considers the role of PFI and the next chapter that of DFI (and quasi-DFI) inflows in Korea.

A.   The Potential of Portfolio Foreign Investment

3.02   Foreign portfolio investment is an important source of foreign capital which has not been tapped to any significant degree in Korea. Meanwhile, individual equity markets are rapidly being "internationalized" due to improved communications, better available information and the continued search for higher returns and portfolio diversification. As part of this phenomenon, international investor interest in Korea is growing, as witnessed by the strong showing of the Korea Fund on the New York stock exchange over the past two years. An opportunity exists for Korea at the present time to take advantage of prevailing investor confidence to expand its use of equity funding, an opportunity that it should not ignore.

3.03   Advantages of Portfolio Foreign Investment. Portfolio foreign investment, first of all, offers diversification through the opportunity to raise additional long-term funds from a new pool of capital--primarily institutional investors abroad. That pool is considerable and growing rapidly. Moreover, the nature of institutional investment is attractive; it generally seeks long-term capital gains appreciation, rather than short-term gains. Also, in contrast to foreign direct investment, the motive of such investment is portfolio returns, not control. Once diversification through internationalization begins, it can be self-fulfilling. The more Korean companies are known by foreign portfolio investors and in different capital markets, the more opportunities for greater access to funding sources. The experience of the Japanese since the mid-1970s is a pertinent reminder of the gains from liberalizing corporate access to international capital markets and investors. It has improved stock valuations and dramatically increased the funding options of Japanese companies, especially medium-sized, high-growth companies.

3.04   Second, foreign portfolio investment represents risk capital rather than inflexible debt capital. Greater reliance on equity capital, both domestic and foreign, would help strengthen the capital base of Korean industry, improve its financial flexibility and thus its capacity to withstand adverse industry or economy-wide shocks. Debt capital must be serviced no matter what the profitability or cash flow situation of a company (and country). Equity capital earns rent only when the firm generates profits and at the discretion of corporate management; in that sense, it is a more flexible, reliable source of funding. The corporate finance literature is filled with discussions on the debt vs. equity trade-off. Whether one relies more on debt or equity depends on the relative tax-adjusted cost of each financing instrument and the risk and profit characteristics of the business concerned. Financial flexibility is essential in an environment like that of Korea's corporate sector, where the growth of exports and corporate revenue are especially vulnerable to rapid changes in international demand and market competitiveness, where profit margins remain low and where a strong corporate funding capability is essential to assure financing for continued expansion. Greater use of equity would strengthen corporate balance sheets, thus expanding firms' capacity to fund long-term capital and research spending. Also, just by reducing interest expense, it could help to improve corporate profitability, augmenting retained earnings and internal sources of funds. Healthier corporate balance sheets would then alleviate pressure on the banking system and ultimately on the government by reducing the need to assist financially distressed companies.

3.05   Third, internationalization could have a demonstration or feedback effect. Exposure to foreign markets and investors could help to encourage a stronger, more developed stock market, with benefits to the capital market as a whole. It would do so by encouraging competition, market-oriented pricing, improved disclosure standards and more sophisticated industry and company analytical techniques. Moreover, foreign investors could provide market feedback; in some cases, they might see the growth potential of Korean firms more clearly from abroad.

3.06   Fourth, foreign portfolio investment may help to enhance market valuations and prospects for higher capital gains by injecting further demand into the market. Those stock markets which have been more open to foreign portfolio investment have seen remarkable growth in market capitalization through higher share values. As confidence develops that strong future gains are possible, further investors are attracted. And higher share valuations stimulate equity issues--by lowering the cost of equity to a firm and creating incentives for reluctant owners to go public.

3.07   Finally, a stronger equity market--supported by foreign portfolio investment and enhanced domestic investor interest--provides an environment where an active over-the-counter market, accessible to relatively small- or medium-sized companies, could also develop and flourish under an appropriate regulatory framework. It also makes it easier to raise equity capital for new companies, since venture capital companies seem to do best in countries with active stock markets, where a successful new venture may more readily be divested profitably through a public offering.

3.08   The Pool of Foreign Portfolio Investment. In recent years, institutional investors, particularly the US and European pension funds, have dramatically increased their investments in international securities. This is due to the large amounts of capital they have accumulated and continue to accumulate, their ongoing need for portfolio diversification, and their continuing search for undiscovered markets and higher returns. The foreign commitments of US pension funds reached an estimated $16 billion at the end of 1984--more than double their level only two years earlier. At the end of

1982, foreign equity investments of British and other European pension funds represented 15% and 8.5%, respectively, of total portfolios equivalent to $100 billion and $335 billion; that proportion has risen since, in the British case to perhaps as much as 25%.[34] Japanese pension funds, which since 1979 have been allowed to place up to 10% of their funds in foreign assets, by 1985 had placed abroad about 8% of total assets (equivalent to over $55 billion).

3.09   The OECD countries have been the primary beneficiaries of this surge in interest by international investors. Japan, which liberalized its market only relatively recently, has also taken advantage of this phenomenon. Japanese companies, for example, have raised over $2 billion in new capital through foreign issues since the mid-1960s.[35] The Tokyo stock market has benefited from inflows of capital from American pension funds, European institutional investors and OPEC countries seeking to diversify away from dollar-denominated investments.

3.10   The principal beneficiaries among developing countries have been Hong Kong, Malaysia, Singapore and Israel. The first three of these markets are completely open to foreign investors, while Israel's market is considered relatively free. Stimulated by foreign investment, the growth of these markets has occurred primarily through capital increases and growth in earnings of already listed companies, rather than through government incentives to promote new listings. An informal estimate of total foreign equity investment in markets of developing countries is US$700-750 million, which is still very small.[36] But the potential is significant; much will depend on the policies of host countries to open up equity markets and promote the availability of good corporate information.

3.11   Surveys indicate there is considerable openmindedness among institutional investors towards portfolio investment in developing countries. Some investors take the position that the rewards of careful, discriminating investment in certain developing countries outweigh the risks. Some would place 1-2% of their portfolios in LDC markets, just as they invest a small percentage in venture capital funds. The annual increase in foreign portfolio investment worldwide is projected to reach over $10 billion by the end of the decade. Of this between $1 and $2 billion could easily flow to developing countries should they provide an accommodating environment.[37] Continued high rates of economic growth in many newly industrialized countries offer the potential of higher rates of return on their corporate stocks than those realizable in OECD countries, where potential growth may be lower. The desire to stabilize returns (reduce variance) through portfolio diversification

---

34/ Lessard and Williamson (1985).

35/ Barth and Wall (1985). The Japanese experience with capital market liberalization is discussed in Appendix 3B.

36/ Lessard and Williamson (1985).

37/ Lessard and Williamson (1985).

should also contribute to future demand for the equities of countries such as Korea.

B. The Development of the Korean Equity Market

3.12   Traditional Reliance on Debt Financing. Traditionally, the Korean government has played a very activist role in corporate finance -- through financial policy and directed lending via the banking system (at one time largely government-controlled). Interest rate ceilings during the 1970s reduced the cost of debt, making it attractive for the corporate sector to rely on debt financing to fund its rapid expansion. The real cost of bank loans was, in fact, negative during most of the 1970s for both domestic and foreign loans.

3.13   In addition, a number of the larger preferred industries were favored with loans through directed credit programs at further preferential rates, sometimes irrespective of their underlying competitiveness or the profitability of a specific investment. This further increased corporate access, particularly of the larger companies, to debt finance; ironically, some of the more established companies would have been obvious candidates to raise capital through the fledgling equity market. There was also a presumption that companies, at least in preferred industries, would be bailed out by the government-supported banks if they encountered financial problems. This reduced the perceived riskiness of debt finance.

3.14   Moreover, there was heavy reliance on foreign borrowing, channeled through the banking system since domestic savings alone were not large enough to fuel the economic expansion. The combination of low interest rates abroad (especially in the late 1960s), tight credit rationing domestically and the import privileges of exporters produced a strong demand for foreign loans that was difficult to control.

3.15   As a result of the above-mentioned factors, an environment was created which tolerated high corporate debt-to-equity ratios and company debt structures heavily weighted towards the short term. There was little or no incentive to raise investment capital through the equity market. Consequently, the corporate debt/equity ratio increased significantly throughout the 1970s to over four to one by 1980 (see Table 3.1).

Table 3.1: COMPARATIVE DEBT - EQUITY RATIOS (Manufacturing Sector)

Countries	1974	1976	1978	1980	1982	1983
Korea	n.a.	3.65	3.67	4.88	3.86	3.60
USA	0.88	0.86	0.93	1.01	1.06	1.04
Japan	n.a.	n.a.	n.a.	3.85	3.92	3.24
Germany	1.96	2.12	2.09	2.14	2.16	2.18

3.16   The lack of accountability created by government control of financial intermediation also inhibited the quality of credit assessment, efficiency and product development of the banking system, as well as the independence and diversification of the financial sector as a whole. As in Japan up until the mid-1970s, the predominant role of indirect finance resulted in delaying the development of meaningful alternatives to banks for both borrowers and investors.

3.17   Regulatory policies, institutional constraints and traditional practices have also constrained demand and supply in both primary and secondary markets. Some of the major factors affecting the supply of stock issues have been the high financial cost of raising equity and the negative attitude of private owners towards sharing ownership and control. Two government policies--concerning pricing and dividends--in particular adversely affected the cost of issuing equity; they are now being progressively eased.

3.18   Up until 1984, all stocks were issued at par value, irrespective of true market value. Firms, whose stock value had appreciated in the market, were issuing stocks at an undervalued price. This prevented owners and existing shareholders from enjoying capital gains that might have accompanied the rapid expansion of the economy. Further dampening the interest of potential issuing companies was the fact that low prices also meant they had to offer a larger number of shares to raise a desired amount of funds. This diluted the original owner's control and ultimately added to the dividend burden. At the other extreme, firms with shares at market values considerably below par found it extremely difficult to issue new shares at par.

3.19   The government also used its influence to set dividend rates, specified as a percentage of par value and aligned closely to long-term deposit rates. In this environment, stocks took on the characteristics of bonds-- bought and sold on the basis of yield (the dividend), rather than capital gains based on the earnings and growth potential of each firm. It also prevented the buildup of equity by firms. Both these practices failed to provide incentives for firms to list their shares or float new issues voluntarily, constricting the volume and value of the market, and reinforced their inclination for debt financing.

3.20   Growth in the Domestic Bond Market. Meanwhile, alternative funding through commercial banks, non-bank financial intermediaries, the curb market and corporate bond issues was easily available, with no loss of control and often at lower cost (considering virtually mandatory dividend payments on an after tax basis for equity vs. tax deductions and guarantees available for some types of debt). In fact, as financial liberalization in the 1980s encouraged diversification from straight bank lending, the corporate sector has increasingly relied on debt securities for fund raising. The major surge in funding during the last five years has been through the domestic bond market. The trend in bond issues relative to equity issues is dramatic: of corporate funds raised through the securities market in 1978, 50% came from equity issues and 50% from bond issues; by 1984, despite a slump in the bond market that year, 79% of funds came from bond issues vs. 21% for equity issues (see Table 3.2). The value of secondary bond trading has also increased exceeding trading in shares.

Table 3.2: FUNDS RAISED THROUGH SECURITIES MARKET

| | Stock | | Bond | | Total |
	Amount (bil. Won)	Component Ratio (%)	Amount (bil. Won)	Component Ratio (%)	Amount (bil. Won)
1975	122.80	78.6	33.45	21.4	156.26
1976	175.95	67.1	86.28	32.9	262.23
1977	185.97	51.3	175.48	48.7	362.45
1978	326.72	50.0	326.34	50.0	653.06
1979	216.80	25.8	624.63	74.2	841.43
1980	171.15	15.1	963.70	84.9	1,134.85
1981	306.04	22.8	1,036.15	77.2	1,342.19
1982	276.87	11.6	2,112.17	88.4	2,389.04
1983	462.57	24.5	1,426.52	75.5	1,889.09
1984	479.06	21.0	1,804.06	79.0	2,283.12

Source: Securities Supervisory Board, Seoul, Korea.

3.21   Yet the corporate bond market as presently constituted is very limited and does not offer diversified, long-term financing. Despite efforts to liberalize the market over the past four years,[38] there is little differentiation among bond issues; most bonds still are issued on standard terms and conditions, with maturities being only 3-5 years. Moreover, the majority of bonds continue to be issued with financial guarantees from banks, thus perpetuating reliance on the banking system. Unguaranteed bonds today make up less than 10% of new bond issues. Bank guarantees of bond issues create a bias towards bonds relative to stocks as they lower the risk of the former. This dampens investor interest in equities--at a time when that market offers the only source of flexible, long-term financing.

3.22   Potential of the Stock Market. The Korean government began to encourage the growth of the equity market in the late 1960s. The Korean Stock Exchange (KSE) was established in February 1956, but activity was very slow until the government took measures to encourage businesses to go public through preferential tax measures and some jawboning. Through additional legislation in 1972, the government put pressure on firms to go public, again supported by incentives in tax and financing areas. All of these measures led to a rapid expansion of the market. But by the early 1980s, interest in the equity market had leveled off--in part, because tax incentives were reduced

---

38/ The government recently liberalized conditions of bond issuance, urging companies to issue new types of bonds -- unguaranteed bonds, convertible bonds, bonds with warrants, etc. Since 1981, it has also allowed some flexibility in the determination of corporate bond rates within a range of 2% above and below a base rate.

substantially as a result of tax reform in 1978 and, in part, because of the economic downturn and some incidents of insider trading in the securities markets.

3.23   Because of the improved economic outlook and recent measures by the government, stock market activity has improved since 1984, with an upsurge in activity in 1986. Various measures taken by the Ministry of Finance in 1985 contributed to the stronger interest in the market: reduction of taxes on dividends for small private investors; liberalization of listing requirements; lower margin requirements; encouragement of equity purchases by institutional investors; and increases in permitted foreign portfolio investment (through new investment trusts). The sharp improvement in Korea's economic fundamentals has probably been the most important factor behind the stock market's bullish rally through most of 1986.

3.24   Still, despite recent strength in the Korean stock market, the potential of the market is much greater. Its overall size, volume of activity and valuation remain low in comparison with US, Japanese or major European exchanges. On the supply side, according to several observers, there are over a hundred significant companies which could go public immediately. Indeed, over 800 companies have issued corporate bonds compared with, at the peak, 356 companies issuing equity. Hence, there is greater scope for increasing new issues of equities. The government's recent liberalization of listing requirements--now only a minimum of 20% of equity must be issued for a listing in the second trading tier of the KSE--should help stimulate new issues by offering companies the flexibility to issue shares without losing control. In many cases, however, even when a company is publicly listed, most of its shares are unavailable for public trading as they are closely held by the original owners or "insiders." Much of recent issue activity has in fact, been through rights issues (sales of shares exclusively to existing shareholders). This affects the "float"--the number of shares available to the general public and outside institutional investors for trading. This practice restricts the growth and liquidity of the market.

3.25   Low share valuation is a serious problem in Korea, and it perpetuates the trend of low new issue activity mentioned above. Table 3.3 compares company listings and market capitalizations of several different countries. Korea's market capitalization is low relative to countries with a similar or lower number of listings. It is also low relative to GDP and volume of financial assets. Korea's P/E ratio has been about 5.2 times earnings although because of recent interest it has moved up to 7-8 in 1986. This compares poorly with P/E ratios of 25 in Japan, 10 in Hong Kong, 14 in London and 13.7 in the United States (1984/85 data). This is surprising considering the strength of the Korean economy. With specific efforts to strengthen the domestic equity market and encourage investor demand, the valuation of Korean shares should tend to move towards international levels--to at least 10 times earnings. As private entrepreneurs see the opportunity for significant capital gains, they will then have greater incentive to go public or issue shares to outside parties.

3.26   Less than 2% of the economically active population in Korea invests in stocks, compared to 10% in developed countries. Individual investors shy away from the market because of its perceived riskiness, sluggish secondary market which affects liquidity, lack of corporate information and lack of information generally about operations of the stock market. Also, institutional investors, which are the driving force in most developed country stock markets, are still relatively inactive in Korea's stock market. Thus the potential for increasing demand in the stock market is substantial. Increased foreign portfolio investment would supplement and indeed could encourage domestic demand. Broader participation, along with regulatory improvements, would reduce the likelihood of boom and bust cycles which have occurred in the Korean stock market. As potential investors see profitable opportunities and gain confidence in the market, they will be wooed away from other investments such as the bond market or the traditionally attractive real estate and curb markets.

Table 3.3: STOCK MARKET DATA FOR SELECTED COUNTRIES, 1984

	No. of Listed Companies	Market Capitalization (US$ billion)	Market capitalization/GDP (%)
Mature Markets			
New York (NYSE)	1,490	1,530.0	42
Tokyo	1,427	644.0	51
London	2,171	243.0	57
Toronto	943	135.0	40
Germany	449	78.0	13
Australia	1,009	49.9	27
Stockholm	159	25.7	28
Brussels	197	12.2	16
Copenhagen	231	7.6	14
Developing Markets			
Malaysia	278	15.3	53
Brazil	608	28.9	15
India	3,882	7.9	5
Korea	336	6.1	7
Thailand	89	1.7	4
Argentina	236	1.2	2
Indonesia	24	0.1	0.1

Source: International Finance Corporation.

Note: The market capitalization to GDP ratios for mature markets are biased downward to the extent that multiple stock markets may exist in those countries; this applies particularly to the US where markets other than the NYSE account for a substantial chunk of total market capitalization.

3.27   Korea's Internationalization Policy.   Spurred by the need to diversify funding and liberalize its financial sector, the Korean government has already taken significant steps to open its equity market to international investors.   In 1981, it introduced a four-stage plan for internationalization to be implemented over ten years:

(a)   The first stage permitted indirect securities investment by foreigners.   This has occurred through investment trusts established in Seoul over the past four years (now five trusts are operating) and the Korea Fund which was listed on the New York Stock Exchange two years ago.   Foreign securities firms have also been allowed to make limited investments in domestic securities firms and to open representative offices in Korea, although they are not yet permitted to conduct domestic business.

(b)   The second stage of liberalization, announced in November 1985, permits domestic companies to issue convertible debt securities on international markets under guidelines set by the government.

(c)   The third stage, due by the late 1980s, would allow foreigners to make unlimited investments in Korean securities.   Korean securities would also be listed on overseas stock exchanges, and the government would permit limited securities business by securities firms abroad on the basis of reciprocity.

(d)   The fourth and final stage is presently targeted for the early 1990s.   At that time, domestic investors would be allowed to invest in foreign securities, and foreign securities could be listed on the Korean exchange.   There would be no-limit liberalization of securities business by securities firms at home and abroad.

3.28   Stage one has been very successful in terms of attracting investor interest.   Two open-ended investment trusts for the issuance of beneficial certificates for foreigners were established in 1981 with initial limits of $15 million each.   The performance of both trusts was good, and in 1983 each trust was increased by $10 million, bringing total funds to $50 million. Three additional funds were established in 1985 with total funding of $90 million (see Table 3.4).   These trusts are now fully subscribed, but so far the government has not granted another increase in capital.

3.29   The Korea Fund, Inc., a closed-end investment company registered with the USSEC and listed on the NYSE, invests primarily in Korean stocks; it began with an original public offering of $60 million in August 1984.   Since then the stock has typically traded at a hefty premium over net asset value (about 75% at one stage) and a new tranche of $40 million was successfully launched in mid-1986.[39]

3.30   Stage two was initiated in November 1985 when the government announced that Korean companies with net assets exceeding 50 billion won (about $56.8 million at that time) and stock yielding dividends of more than 20% were allowed to issue convertible securities in international money markets; some 16 companies presently meet these criteria. Three companies (Samsung Electronics, Daewoo Heavy and Yukong) have since issued convertible debentures in the cumulative amount of $80 million. Each issue was priced at what appeared to seasoned market participants to be the issuer's advantage but, because of the scarcity of Korean equities in international markets, was fully subscribed with ease. A number of international investment companies are now eager to participate in underwriting issues by other Korean firms.

Table 3.4: PORTFOLIO FOREIGN INVESTMENT IN KOREA

Fund	Amount ($ million)	Date of establishment
Korea International Trust	25	Nov. 1981
Korea Trust	25	Nov. 1981
Korea Fund /a	100	Aug. 1984; Apr. 1986
Korea Growth Trust	30	Mar. 1985
Seoul International Trust	30	Apr. 1985
Seoul Trust	30	Apr. 1985
Venture Fund	5	Dec. 1985; Apr. 1986
Convertible Debentures /b	80	Dec. 1985-May 1986
Total	325	

/a   Including second tranche of $40 million launched in April 1986.
/b   Comprising issuances of three private companies: Samsung Electronics ($20 million); Daewoo Heavy ($40 million) and Yukong ($20 million).

C. Further Promotion of Foreign Portfolio Investment

3.31   The step by step approach taken by Korea is sound and reasonable. However, given the initial interest shown in the first two stages of Korea's

---

39/   The International Finance Corporation (IFC), the private sector oriented component of the World Bank, has been instrumental in launching both tranches of the Korea Fund and in supporting measures, such as the establishment of a domestic bond rating agency, to promote the development of the Korean securities market.

internationalization plan and the need for long-term funding and diversification away from debt, Korean authorities ought to consider stepping up the pace of liberalization to take advantage of the favorable investment climate, particularly at this point when the country's trade position is strong.

3.32   Korea's investment trusts and overseas funds, as well as issuance of convertible bonds by Korean firms in international markets function as bridges to the domestic equity market. They create familiarity with the Korean corporate names and even generate healthy corporate publicity. The government could promote internationalization by expanding participation in the various investment trusts operating on the KSE. The success of the Korea Fund has created interest among underwriters and fund managers to undertake similar efforts in the US market and elsewhere. Additional funds similar to the Korea Fund could be established on other exchanges abroad to tap interest in those markets.[40]

3.33   The second phase of internationalization could also be promoted further. Korean firms should be encouraged to issue convertible bonds in the Euromarkets--with appropriate pricing and straightforward conversion features. The process of tapping international securities markets by corporate names should even go a stage further in the next few years through issues by a greater number of companies in a number of different currencies. The Japanese experience with convertible bonds issued in the Euromarkets has been a positive one.

3.34   The government should also now consider allowing the issuance of foreign depository receipts as a way of attracting further overseas portfolio investment. American depository receipts (ADRs), for example, are vehicles by which shares of foreign companies can be traded in dollar denominations and in bearer form in the US domestic market. They are used for the trading of

---

[40] Of course, the establishment of stock funds abroad is also dependent on the rules and regulations of the particular exchanges involved. It may also be argued that, with the opening of the Seoul stock exchange to direct purchase of Korean stocks by foreigners within a few years there should no longer be a need for Korean stock funds in overseas markets. This overlooks the psychology of international investors, however, particularly that of smaller individual investors who are much more comfortable in purchasing stocks on local exchanges.

shares in companies based particularly in Europe and East Asia. This system has grown rapidly in recent years.[41]

3.35   After further expanding the first two phases, the government should consider advancement of phase three of its internationalization program. It could do this by promoting better acceptance of foreign portfolio investment and by undertaking measures to strengthen the domestic capital market.

3.36   <u>Overcoming Reservations Concerning PFI</u>: One of the main constraints to direct portfolio investment in developing countries arises from fear of "creeping control." This concern is often exaggerated. Unlike direct investment, portfolio investment usually means minority investment; it is aimed at an attractive financial return rather than control. As mentioned earlier, the principal sources of foreign capital are pension funds, which are not interested in the responsibility of control and in fact rarely vote the shares they do hold. They tend to limit their holdings in any one enterprise to 2-5% of outstanding stock, in order to minimize risk and avoid difficulty in selling. This is the type of capital in which Korea should be most interested.

3.37   Additional safeguards can be instituted, however. Korea already has placed restrictions on the level of foreign portfolio investment in individual Korean companies and industries permitted to the various stock funds so far established. Other countries have taken pragmatic steps to allow free equity markets but at the same time to minimize possible foreign control. Germany, for example, limits the extent of foreign control of domestic companies by creating separate classes of shares. Ordinary shares have voting rights; preferred shares do not, but instead their claim on dividends is a cumulative one and takes precedence over that of ordinary shareholders. Foreign investors are allowed to invest in preferred shares only.

3.38   Sweden, in 1982, created "free shares" which are available to foreign investors. Creation of these shares was the result of a major change in legislation to allow non-residents greater access to the Swedish equity

---

41/   To create an ADR, the shares of a company are purchased on the local exchange in question and held in safe custody; the custodian is normally a bank. The bank then issues a certificate which represents the shares in question. The certificate usually represents a package of shares which brings the value of the certificate in line with the value of actively traded shares in the U.S. domestic market. Certificates are denominated in dollars and traded as a security in their own right. Any market maker in the "over the counter" market in the US will deal in ADRs on behalf of its client. The possible disadvantage of ADRs is that they effectively turn registered shares into bearer shares; therefore, a company cannot trace the ownership of its shares. Limits on the amount of equity held in the form of ADRs can, however, prevent concentration of ownership. Up to 20% of equity in individual companies has been held in the form of ADRs.

market.[42/] Companies are required to obtain special permission from the central bank to issue free shares, but all major companies, except banks and certain other specified companies which cannot have foreign ownership, have been granted this permission. There is a limit to the amount of free shares a company can issue. In most cases this is up to 20% of its voting capital. Most free shares, however, are issued as so-called "B" shares, which hold reduced voting power (1/10 of a vote). Therefore, it would be possible for a company to sell, say, 40% of its equity abroad but less than 20% of voting shares. During 1982 and 1983, more than SKr 7 billion of shares were sold to foreigners through this instrument.

3.39   There is also concern expressed that foreign investors will be buying shares in domestic companies at unfairly low prices. Low share valuation is often caused by restraints on or insulation of equity markets. Foreign portfolio investment should, in fact, help to raise share valuations by injecting greater demand; as mentioned earlier, this would stimulate capital gains for existing domestic investors and company owners and, in turn, stimulate new equity issues if priced at market.

3.40   A variant of the low price argument is the contention that Korean firms will have to offer high yields to foreign investors in order to attract and keep them and this will eat into retained earnings and damage the prospects of company expansion. While, in general, it is correct to expect that equity investors will require higher compensation in the long run than debt-lenders because of their assumption of greater risk, this does not necessarily mean that company expansion has to be sacrificed. Higher returns can be offered in the form of capital gains and investors may indeed be positively inclined towards firms whose dividends are kept low because earnings are plowed back into company expansion. Furthermore, many investors will be attracted even if dividend return is low provided the stock helps them reduce their overall risk. Studies show that despite their lower-than-average return Korean stocks would be preferred by US investors because of their risk diversification characteristics (Anckonie and Chi, 1986).

3.41   Finally, another concern is the possible volatility of foreign portfolio investment, creating sudden shifts of flows in and out of the stock market, and the related effect on the currency. Indeed, there are swings in stock market activity. But share price volatility is often most extreme in thinly capitalized stock markets with narrow ownership, which can lead to insider trading. To the extent that diversification of sources of capital creates a broader market, foreign portfolio investment could actually foster greater liquidity and stability. Also, in practice most foreign institutional

---

42/   The experience of Sweden may offer a useful parallel for Korea. Around 1980-81, the Swedish government realized its domestic stock market was not mature enough to give full valuation to its companies; thus companies were encouraged to issue primary shares in London or New York. This stimulated overall market valuations and later stock market activity at home, by drawing attention to the investment opportunities in the domestic market.

investors establish minimum and maximum exposure levels by country, industry and individual company. Changes in portfolio composition often occur by not making new investments from net available cash flow, rather than from net disinvestment. Moreover, there is some evidence that foreign portfolio investment is countercyclical.

3.42   Also, investor interest depends on a positive view of the domestic economy, the domestic capital market and the individual company. Foreign investors are presently attracted to Korean stocks because of the strength of the Korean economy and the healthy prospects of individual companies. To the extent that greater access to equity further enhances corporate financial health and expands the availability of long-term funding for needed economic expansion, investor optimism should be reinforced.

3.43   Strengthening the Domestic Securities Market: The Korean capital market suffers, at present, from a number of shortcomings which are being overlooked by international investors rushing to get a piece of a product in scarce supply. Once Korean equities are freely available to those investors the extent of foreign interest in them will be largely determined by the scope and pace of measures undertaken to strengthen and reform the domestic capital market. In the long run, the most effective way of making Korean equities more acceptable internationally will be to make them more acceptable domestically. Measures which Korea ought to consider now to strengthen the domestic capital market to facilitate greater foreign and domestic portfolio investment include:[43]

> (a) Pricing and Dividend Policies: Since par value reference pricing has no economic significance the government should discourage it. The level and quality of earnings should be the main determinants of issue price. The practice of linking dividends to par value should also be discouraged. Individual companies should have complete flexibility in determining dividends on the basis of corporate profits and investment needs.

> (b) Technical Changes: Allowing stock splitting, thus lowering the average stock price, would broaden the market by enabling more individual investors to purchase stocks. Facilitating block trading would also encourage market development. The capitalization of the Korea Securities Finance Corporation (KSFC) could be expanded so as to enable it to undertake this function until individual securities houses are strong enough to do so. Over-the-counter trading should also be encouraged to facilitate the supply of capital to small and medium companies. Again, since Korean securities houses do not yet have the capital to make a stable and sustainable OTC market, the ability of the KSFC to support such trading might be enhanced.

43/ These measures are more fully described and discussed in Appendix 3A.

(c) Regulatory Measures: These would include enhanced disclosure and more standardized accounting practices, more competitive underwriting procedures, stronger investor protection measures, enhanced regulation enforcement powers for the KSE, and training to enhance professionalism and technical capabilities in the operation and overview of securities markets.

(d) Enhancing Domestic Demand: Domestic institutional investors such as pension funds, insurance companies and mutual funds play a significant role in mobilizing savings and promoting the domestic stock market in many countries. To the extent that regulations prevent them from doing the same in Korea there is a case for regulatory reform. Public education as to the role and advantages of securities can also be useful in enhancing demand.

(e) Bond Market Measures: To alleviate the bias against equity further government efforts are needed to promote the use of non-guaranteed bonds. At present bank-guaranteed bonds serve essentially as surrogate loans. The use of credit ratings should also be promoted so as to bring about more efficient pricing relative to risk and increase corporate financial discipline.

- 61 -

KOREA

Appendix 3A: Strengthening the Domestic Securities Market

1.   The importance of developing the domestic capital market appears to
be generally accepted by Government. This is clearly evident in the guidelines for capital market development contained in the Sixth Plan. Among other
objectives, the Plan seeks to facilitate the raising of capital through direct
finance in the corporate sector. Towards this end the Plan seeks to
(i) sharply increase the supply of tradable securities (through tax and
financial reform); (ii) raise investor confidence by means of exercising
stringent control over trading and requiring improvements in corporate
accounting practices; (iii) increase the variety of securities to meet
investor and issuer preference (e.g., preferred stock, convertible bonds);
(iv) reduce the bias in favor of issuing government guaranteed bonds so as to
promote a viable, self-sustaining bond market; (v) enhance the underwriting
role of securities companies and to broaden the range of business activities
open to such companies. Government objectives are expressed in general terms
in the Sixth Plan. Specific actions need to be taken, however, if these
objectives are to be realized. The remainder of this appendix discusses some
specific measures that are required for the strengthening of the domestic
capital market. They fall into several categories, listed below as (i)
Pricing and Technical Changes, (ii) Institutional Measures, (iii) Market
Development Measures, and (iv) Bond Market Improvement Measures.

(a) Pricing and Technical Changes

2.   Pricing and Dividend Policies. Past restrictions on issuance prices
of new stocks have been progressively relaxed over the past few years: now
issues can theoretically be priced at market and companies are permitted to
offer 100% of new shares at market prices (up from 40% previously). Nevertheless, the infrequency with which market-price issues have actually been
floated during the past three years and the continuing "guidance" role of
securities regulators in this regard suggests that the idea of market-pricing
as opposed to par-value pricing has not yet become firmly rooted. Since par
value pricing has no economic significance, the government should now
encourage full liberalization of pricing--to build a system whereby the level
and quality of earnings are the main determinants of pricing for new issues
and where market value underpins the pricing of rights issues.

3.   Dividends still tend to be paid at a certain percentage of par
rather than in consideration of profitability and corporate policy.   Individual companies should have complete flexibility in determining dividends on the
basis of profits. Greater education and further government promotion is
needed to encourage investors to look for potential capital gains rather than
annual income.

4.   Other Technical Changes. Other changes could also stimulate greater
participation in the market. For example, allowing stock splitting, thus
lowering the average stock price, would broaden the market by enabling more
individual investors to afford the investment in equities. Stock splitting

tends to raise market valuations and facilities diversification. It could also have the positive effect of reducing the sanctity of par value. In London, the average stock price is $2.50; thus 100 shares cost, on average, $250.00, an amount accessible to small investors. Korea's average stock price is double that, despite a lower per capita income.

5.   Facilitating block trading would encourage market development. The role of the Korea Securities Finance Corporation (KSFC) as a market maker could be expanded, taking on a more innovative role. The KSE is currently limited by having no ability to cross blocs of shares at negotiated prices within the market. In other countries, brokers are expected to perform this function outside the market, but a shortage of capital limits the ability of Korean houses to perform this function well. KSFC presently has the capital, reputation and related expertise to undertake this role in an expanded way until securities houses are strong enough to do so. Such activity also needs to be well regulated to prevent manipulation.

6.   Over-the-counter (OTC) trading is a natural extension of such a function and is important particularly for small to medium, high-growth companies seeking to raise equity. OTC markets have developed in parallel with most stock exchanges with security companies building up an inventory of unlisted stocks which they buy and sell for their own account. Relatively smaller companies use this market because it avoids listing costs and demands less disclosure. The bulk of shares in stock markets are traded over the counter (although the value of turnover on the exchanges is higher because of the larger companies listed on the exchanges). Development of OTC trading makes sense given the government's interest in facilitating the supply of capital for small- and medium-size high technology manufacturing companies. OTC trading in Korea, as it exists presently, is dominated by bond transactions rather than equities. Since Korean securities houses do not have the capital to make a dynamic OTC market in equities at present, KSFC might seek to expand its support to this activity.

7.   Efforts to assure good back-office functions, automation, communications and custodial functions are also extremely important, particular to foreign investors, in order to avoid any settlement problems.

   (b) Institutional Measures

8.   There are several institutional changes which could promote a healthier equity market as well as encourage foreign portfolio investment. These include improved disclosure and accounting practices and introduction of corporate information services; an improved underwriting system including greater foreign participation; further development of the regulatory structure; and, finally, continued public education and training to enhance professionalism and technical capabilities in the operation and overview of securities markets.

9.   Disclosure and Accounting. Adequate accounting and auditing are at the heart of a properly functioning financial system. Investor confidence in both the securities and equities markets in Korea would be boosted by greater availability of corporate financial information--from independent sources and through improved, standardized accounting practices.

10.   In the absence of integrated, timely and reliable corporate information, both initial corporate issues and development of a secondary market are impeded, affecting the size and liquidity of the market. Under the supervision of the Securities Exchange Commission and its Securities Supervisory Board (SEC/SSB), steps have already been taken to require listed companies to publish reports, but the information may not always be sufficient to enable investors to make informed judgments. The production of better company information under the supervision of the SEC/SSB also needs to be supported by a more effective system of disseminating that information. Development of independent corporate information and analytical services also must be encouraged. Furthermore, in many Western countries, it is common for company officers to give regular briefings to investment analysts, to develop fuller appreciation of the company and its financial position. This practice could be encouraged in Korea. Better disclosure will develop also as companies realize it is in their own interests as an aid to raising cheaper funds in the securities markets.

11.   The accounting and auditing industry is also relatively new in Korea, and there is an insufficient supply of accountants. Greater attention is needed to developing further a professional accounting association for certification and licensing, development of uniform accounting principles and auditing standards and establishment of standards for financial reporting. The Korean government may want to consider sponsoring a study by a qualified outside firm to suggest ways to encourage development of the industry and improve accounting and auditing standards.

12.   Certain specific improvements in corporate accounting could enhance the analysis and valuation of companies. First, traditional accounting methods have tended to obscure information on consolidated companies, particularly the status of intercompany loans and equity investments. When intercompany relationships are not specifically spelled out in audited financial statements, the result is uncertainty in the minds of investors as to the true state of affairs of a company or group of companies. Improved disclosure could help boost investor confidence. Second, Korean firms do not fully adjust the value of their assets to reflect inflation, thus fixed assets can be undervalued, again affecting valuation of the company. In this regard, however, Korean accounting practice is similar to that of many advanced countries and, indeed, better than some (e.g. Japan).

13.   <u>Underwriting System and Development of the Securities Industry</u>. The system suffers from a number of weaknesses resulting from the fact that too little is left to market forces. Securities companies do not compete in all respects for the management of issues. Fees for underwriting and managing issues of both equities and corporate bonds are also fixed by the regulatory authorities instead of by negotiation between the issuer and the management/ underwriting group. The reluctance to price at market also affects the underwriting function. What occurs is that commitments to underwrite are not, in practice, always firm; this allows underwriters to get around pricing guidelines. This further raises the cost of issuance for a company. The lead manager, who is most closely in touch with potential investors, really should have the freedom to work with the company to decide the amount, pricing and fee structure and to form the underwriting group. The government could help

correct the problem by changing the nature of its guidance to underwriting institutions and ultimately allowing greater competition.

14.   There is also merit in promoting some changes in the securities industry. The seven principal securities companies are owned by leading conglomerates; this has helped them to develop an adequate capital base, but it has also contributed to the public perception of insider control of the equity market. It may be appropriate to encourage the dilution of conglomerate ownership in these companies. At the same time, the various companies in the industry (merchant banks, securities companies and finance houses) might be encouraged to form larger groupings in order to obtain economies of management resources and larger capital bases (in order to undertake larger underwriting commitments). This process would be enhanced by the Government moving to a negative list of activities rather than the present positive list which specifically dictates the activities of different companies in the industry. The negative list should be rather short, retaining primarily the basic distinction between commercial and trust banking on the one hand and securities-related business on the other.

15.   Foreign securities companies could play a role in providing capital and management resources as well as the latest financial techniques. Allowing foreign companies to take a significant (though not controlling) shareholding in domestic securities companies could be beneficial, as it would facilitate greater transfer of market know-how. Foreign companies have recently been permitted to take on a total 10% shareholding in Korean securities companies (maximum 5% per investor). This size of holding is probably too low to get the full benefits of foreign involvement in terms of better management, increased capital adequacy and access to more sophisticated market instruments.

16.   Regulatory Concerns. The government has traditionally been heavily involved in the financial and securities markets, because of its desire to support the industrial and export sectors of the economy. It is now gradually moving away from past detailed control to a broader supervisory role. This can only be achieved, however, as these markets strengthen (with institutional changes such as those discussed above) and develop their own self-regulatory capabilities, thus reducing public concern over possible market manipulation. It may be appropriate at this junction, therefore, for the Ministry of Finance to sponsor a review by outside consultants of mechanisms for improved self-regulation of the securities industry as well as for appropriate governmental supervision. Such a review at this time might identify changes or directions for policy which could enhance investor confidence in the market.

17.   Professional Training. Through the Korean Securities Dealers Association (KSDA), a self-regulatory body of brokerage houses, and other auspices, specialized training could be organized for the professionals responsible for the operation and supervision of the securities market. That training could cover analytical techniques for valuing equities and different types of debt securities, analyzing credit risk and evaluating priorities in capital allocation.

(c) Market Development Measures

18.   Use of Tax Incentives to Encourage Issues. The most direct way of stimulating new issues in the market is through tax concessions. Tax incentives accorded in the 1970s helped create the initial surge of the stock market in Korea. They have been progressively removed since 1978, and the difference in corporate taxation between listed and unlisted companies is now only about 3%. Naturally, the tax system should ultimately be neutral between listed and nonlisted companies. Temporary tax discrimination may be justified only to stimulate capital market development and perhaps mitigate other distortions, if the latter cannot be removed directly. The government may want to consider reintroducing tax incentives, perhaps on a temporary and decreasing basis, to encourage companies to go public, if measures on the demand side cannot alone create the incentive to attract companies into the market. Some relief might also be offered on new issues of presently listed companies where the proceeds are used, for example, for new investment in emerging technologies, new product development or export oriented investment.

19.   The government also has a particularly powerful tool in respect of estate taxes. It might consider lifting or delaying such taxes on profits received from primary stock issues. Such an approach would be designed to attract old family or closely held enterprises, who have so far feared going public. One could also consider relaxing estate taxation on money invested in new equity subscriptions or for issues where the proceeds are going to targeted industries. The Cooreman provisions of the Belgian LeClerq law during 1982/83 incorporated such measures. Among other tax advantages, death and gift duties were exonerated for ten years on special shares which were issued to raise capital for investment specifically in Belgium. Such measures were extremely successful in encouraging formation of risk capital.

20.   Attracting New Investors. While the emphasis of this paper is on foreign portfolio investment, there is also considerable scope for further attracting domestic investors to the equity market. There is a much greater role for pension funds, insurance companies and mutual funds, which so far have not been very active in the Korean market, in mobilizing individual savings and channeling them to the equity market. Only about 31% of Korean shares are held by private corporate investors, including insurance companies, although this is up from 15% in 1972. This compares with a current 66% in Japan and 58% in the UK (1984 data). For example, the Japanese insurance market, second largest in the world after the US, is a particularly vital source of long-term funds for Japan's heavy industrial companies and is the country's biggest institutional investor, with 26% of outstanding shares listed on the Tokyo exchange.

21.   The participation of institutional investors, both domestic and foreign, can offer the following advantages: (i) a likely continuous net inflow of new funds to the market; (ii) a core of investors with a long investment horizon, giving the market more stability; (iii) development of professional fund managers, who can evaluate stocks on a more professional basis than individuals generally do; and finally (iv) the institutional base for an increased private placement capability for placing debt of higher-risk or less well-known companies (a vigorous private placement market could pro-

- 66 -

vide a better alternative to the existing curb market). The government therefore, ought to consider measures to stimulate the further proliferation and
financial strength of such institutions, providing them also with greater
flexibility to invest in equities. A step in this direction is the recent
government encouragement of <u>insurance companies</u> to invest a greater share of
funds in equities (September 1985); in the past they have shown greater interest in debt securities.

22.   While the insurance industry has been developing well, thanks to
initial government support, the <u>formation of pension funds</u> is relatively
undeveloped in Korea. The three major funds--for government workers, teachers
and the military--are only partially funded, and just a small percentage is
presently invested in equities. Efforts should be made to fund these pension
plans fully, to develop professional fund management and, finally, to diversify the investments of those funds. There are few pension schemes set up
within companies; the traditional retirement benefit is a lump-sum severance
payment, deducted from a company's current income. For social security
reasons as well as savings accumulation, consideration should be given to
developing funded corporate pension schemes. Given the cash flow constraints
of many Korean companies, implementation would have to be gradual, however.
Alternatively, creation of independent pension schemes could be promoted,
perhaps under the aegis of the insurance companies and funded individually.

23.   <u>Tax deferred retirement and employee savings plans</u> should also be
further encouraged. Existing plans (such as Korea's Employee Savings Plan)
are a good beginning but are not considered to be generous enough to be com-
pelling to potential participants. They might be liberalized further, allowing a higher tax credit for investment in equities. This type of tax incentive program has been successful in mobilizing capital in a number of countries where it has been implemented. The Monory Law in France and similar
measures in Sweden and Belgium are good examples; the Korean government may
want to study these programs carefully.

24.   Sweden, for example, provided considerable impetus to its equity
market by offering incentives to small investors through investment funds.
Individuals subscribe to the funds by paying in regular monthly savings for a
period of five years. The funds, managed by banks and financial institutions,
are invested in the equity market; the individual subscribers benefit not only
from the investment returns but also from special tax concessions. The growth
of these funds were primarily responsible for the strong rise in equity prices
and turnover in Sweden's stock market in 1982/83. Market valuation rose from
SKr 136 billion to SKr 324 billion in the course of six months, and turnover
was the third highest in the world in that year. To moderate that growth, tax
concessions were modified in March 1983, but the funds continue to make a significant contribution to the market.

25.   Further encouragement of existing <u>investment trusts</u> to invest in
Korean equities is needed. Unit trust investment represented less than 5% of
the total domestic equity market in 1983. While there are nine institutions
(three investment trust companies and 6 merchant banks) authorized to undertake the management of unit trusts, only a few are really active. KITC, the
largest operator, invests about 25% of its funds in equities. Because of low

liquidity, it finds it difficult to buy and sell shares without moving the market against itself. This illustrates the need for incentives to expand the number of investors.

26.   Greater efforts should be undertaken to educate and inform the public concerning the advantages of investments in the securities market. A stock market is typically not part of the common tradition of savings and, therefore, this process will take some time. It involves developing financial journalism in publications and on radio and TV; it calls for education at the university and secondary levels; and it demands better individual investor information from the securities industry. As a start, the public needs to understand particularly the advantages of using tax-deferred savings plans and the participatory features of investment trusts, because of the advantages of diversified and long-term investments.

(d) Bond Market Improvements

27.   Policies in the bond market affect the equity market too and there-fore are also considered here. To alleviate the bias against equity, further government efforts are needed to promote faster movement of the bond market away from bank guarantees. Actually, these two sources of long-term funding should be complementary. Active, free-standing and liquid equity and bond markets would both enhance a healthier, diversified corporate finance struc-ture. The experience of the United States is probably the best example of this complementarity because both markets are so fully developed there. Equity is an important source of long-term funding in the United States and provides balance to companies' capitalization structures and needed financial flexibility; the level of equity judged necessary depends on the industry and particular circumstances of the company. Bond financing, however, is the largest source of long-term financing in the United States. But the maturi-ties of those bonds are indeed long-term (up to 30 years), unlike Korean bonds (3-5 years). Furthermore, the variety of instruments in the US bond market and strong secondary markets provide diversity, liquidity and transparency--appealing to both corporate issuers and investors. Instruments are constantly being developed to meet issuers' and market needs. The securitization of debt enables companies to reach directly a broader pool of investors, often at lower initial cost than with loans because the existence of secondary markets offers liquidity to those investors. And, to the issuers, secondary markets provide the discipline, as well as the opportunity, of a continuous market price for their debt instruments.

28.   In Korea, promotion of the equity market should go hand in hand with measures to encourage greater independence and deepening of the domestic bond market--leading to greater innovation and hopefully development of longer-term instruments acceptable to investors. Some of the measures discussed above in the context of equity market development should help: higher disclosure and audit standards, independent corporate information and analytical services, a strong competitive underwriting system and improved regulation.

29.   Use of credit ratings would also facilitate development of a bond market independent of the banking system and government support. Credit ratings benefit the range of participants in financial markets, including

equity investors. They provide an independent assessment of companies and differentiation of credit quality. That encourages more efficient pricing relative to risk. The ratings process also promotes increased disclosure and indeed corporate discipline. It puts pressure on potential issuers to improve their financial structures in order to lower the cost of borrowing. Ratings also can be expected to promote wider underwriting and facilitate placement with investors. Encouragement for the rating and research activities of the one-year-old KBRI and other nascent rating and information services will be extremely important in creating a self-standing domestic securities market.

30. Internationalization of the equity market should also have positive spillover effects in the bond market—by introducing foreign approaches and financial technology as well as competition from expanding funding options. For example, as Korean companies become more comfortable with the issue of convertible bonds abroad, it may encourage them to issue convertible bonds in the domestic market, something which is not commonly done. Convertibles could well be the vehicle by which to encourage companies to enter the domestic equity market and to woo traditional bond investors into equities. The conversion terms could be fixed to encourage maximum conversion at an early date in order to improve debt/equity ratios. The government might consider tax incentives to encourage such issues. Also, internationalization should stimulate the growth and sophistication of the securities industry in Korea, with positive effects on the bond market too, assuming that regulatory changes have been made. Finally, there is a reiterative or self-fulfilling process that goes on. As diversification continues through a stronger, more active equity market and greater access to foreign markets, it should encourage investor confidence and acceptance of other diverse long-term funding instruments, as well as eventually internationalization of Korea's debt securities market too.

- 69 -

KOREA

Appendix 3B: The Japanese Experience with Internationalization

1.   The capital market structures of Japan and Korea, at various points in time and at different stages in their development, have many parallels. Both have relied primarily on indirect finance, usually bank loans, to fund corporate growth—encouraged by the government's interest rate and credit allocation policies. Both governments exercised considerable control, if not ownership, in the financial sector. In Japan, close interlocking relationships were formed between the large city banks and major corporations, assuring easy access to bank funding. In Korea, government control manifested itself through considerable ownership of the banking system. The result in both cases was high debt burdens and less flexible corporate finance. Internal sources of finance, such as retained earnings, were lower, reducing the ability to fund new investment internally. Moreover, control over the financial sector stunted the development of alternative funding sources and instruments. Prior to the 1970s the equity market was very limited. The immaturity of the capital markets contrasted sharply with the growing sophistication of their economies.

2.   Beyond the parallels, however, there also are key differences in Japanese and Korean markets. Japan has a much larger domestic population upon whose savings it can draw. Korea's economy, of necessity, has been much more open. It has had to rely more heavily on foreign debt to finance its development. Its industries are also more dependent on foreign markets than Japanese industries are. And, most importantly, there are different external circumstances facing Korea now, compared with those faced by Japan at a similar stage of development—technological competition and protectionism in the developed markets and cost competition with other newly industrializing countries. Because of these factors, Korea cannot wait as long as Japan did before liberalizing its capital markets. It needs a financial sector which is strong and diversified to meet the funding needs of a growing and increasingly complex industrial structure. It must reduce its high corporate debt in order to achieve greater operating flexibility. And, finally, it needs to diversify its heavy foreign funding away from solely debt financing on which it is running up against the sovereign limits of banks.

3.   Actually, it is the Japanese experience with liberalization of its capital markets over the past 15 years which Korea should consider more carefully. That experience provides some positive feedback concerning the effect of liberalization on corporate finances. In the case of Japan, structural changes in the financial system began in 1974, the year that marked the end of the era of high economic growth and transition to an era of slow growth after the first oil crisis in 1973 and the recession in 1974. Many Japanese companies at that time found themselves overextended, without the ability to weather easily the economic downturn. And the safety net of close banking-corporate relationships showed strain. As one commentator notes: "It became clear that the presence of large loans from city banks was no longer the insurance policy it was once thought to be, as the Daiwa Bank wrote off Eidai Sangyo, a top housing company, the Sumitomo Bank refused new credits to the

- 70 -

trading firm Ataka and Company, and the Dai-Ichi Kangyo Bank refused funds to Kohjin, the textile maker."[4/]

4.   The overwhelming predominance of indirect financing began to lessen gradually from 1974 onwards, as corporations sought to rely further on internal sources of funds and sought external financing increasingly through direct means, such as the issue of straight and convertible bonds and new shares at home and abroad. At the same time, steps were taken to remove or alter regulations relating to interest rates and the scope of financial activities. In fiscal 1970, firms raised 34.5% of long-term funds from internal sources, including retained earnings, depreciation and reserves (Table 3.5). That share had risen to 50.7% by 1979. The share of new external funds raised through direct means stood at 10.4% in fiscal 1973, but had risen to 17.2% by 1980. New share issues in the growing Tokyo stock market doubled to Yen 1,270 billion during the 1970s. During this period, the market also made the important transition from issues of shares at par to issues at market value.

Table 3.5: SOURCES OF LONG-TERM FUNDS RAISED BY JAPANESE CORPORATIONS IN FISCAL 1970 AND 1979

Source	1970	1979
	(Y billion)	
Retained earnings	562	1,465
Depreciation	1,619	2,736
Other internal sources	44	9
Reserves	211	204
Subtotal of internal sources	2,436	4,414
Capital increase (principal)	348	175
Capital increase (surplus)	59	412
Debt securities issued	374	736
Long-term bank loans	132	78
Subtotal of external source	4,059	4,297
Total long-term financing	6,495	8,711
Ratio of internal financing to total	(37.5%)	(50.67%)
Debt securities redeemed	179	546
Long-term loans repaid	1,490	3,856
Net external long-term funds raised	2,390	-105
Net total long-term financing	4,826	4,309
Ratio of interal financing to net total long-term financing	(50.47%)	(102.43%)

Source: Japan Development Bank

4/   Bronte (1982).

5.   One of the most important developments towards the end of the 1970s was the influx of Japanese borrowers into the Euromarkets. The domestic bond market was very restricted for corporate borrowers because of government regulations; Japanese companies were able to replace these sources of funds with securities issued in Europe. In 1977, the Ministry of Finance (MOF) liberalized access to markets by companies of all sizes (prior to that, only a few of the largest and most highly rated companies were allowed to tap the Euromarkets). Decontrol was then finally completed with the enforcement of the new Foreign Exchange and Foreign Trade Control Law in December 1980. The MOF retained the right to monitor the flow of foreign issues through a reporting system.

6.   The reforms created a wave of new issues in Europe. Total bond issues overseas (straight and convertible) surged from $1,495 billion in fiscal 1976 to $3,598 billion in fiscal 1980. Funds raised abroad increased from 0.07% of total external financing in fiscal 1973 to 7.1% by fiscal 1980. The attractions of borrowing in Europe included: more competitive interest rates on foreign funds than often available at home; the opportunity to borrow in foreign currencies, anticipating foreign currency receivables or as a means of diversifying liabilities; publicity and market familiarity for those export-oriented firms listed in foreign securities markets; and, finally, diversity of funding.

7.   In recent years there have been imaginative tailorings of Japanese issues to make them attractive to specific markets. Convertible bonds have been particularly popular with medium-sized, high-growth companies. Since 1977, a large variety of convertible issues have been launched in the Euromarkets; a smaller number of convertible bonds have been floated in the United States. Since 1980, Japanese companies have raised over $20 billion equivalent from the sale of convertible bonds in foreign capital markets.[5]

8.   The change in corporate financing has had a major impact on the Japanese financial system. It has injected new life into the securities markets. It has also improved the depth and trading volume in the domestic Japanese money market. Medium-sized Japanese firms now face a broader range of funding options. A greater number of top-rated Japanese firms, attractive to foreign investors, are offering more new shares for sale. Finally, also, there has been an institutional effect. The process of financial liberalization has moved the balance of power away from the commercial banks, who are now developing new services themselves in order to compete, to the Japanese securities houses which constitute the fastest growing sector of the Japanese financial system. The resulting diversification and specialization offers the impetus to further growth of the financial sector.

9.   This experience suggests that Korea should not wait as long as Japan did before liberalizing and opening its financial sector; indeed, Korea may not be able to afford to, given its dependence on external funding and its continued need for funds to finance corporate growth and technological advancement. Internationalization of its equity market is a key step in this process.

_____

5/   Gill (1985).

IV. FUTURE FINANCING OPTIONS: DIRECT FOREIGN INVESTMENT

A. DFI during the 1970s

4.01   During the 1970s the scale and pattern of DFI in Korea was
controlled by the government through a comprehensive set of guidelines and
regulations. Elaborate criteria were set up to screen DFI applications so as
to keep out projects which might offer significant competition in domestic or
overseas markets to local firms as well as projects which essentially provided
only capital and not much technology. The level of foreign ownership was
effectively limited to 50% by a plethora of guidelines which made it difficult
to obtain approval for a majority foreign owned venture. Furthermore, the
minimum scale of investment was set at $50,000 per project, and gradually
raised to $500,000 in 1979, to prevent small-scale, footloose investments
seeking only to take advantage of Korea's low-cost labor in assembly and
packaging operations. All considered, Korea possessed one of the more
forbidding environments for DFI in this period, especially when compared to
those offered by several other countries in its peer group.

4.02   Because of the discouraging host environment DFI played a relatively
minor role in Korea's development in the 1970s. It typically amounted to less
than 5% of gross foreign capital inflows as compared to 85% for Singapore, 50%
for Kong Kong, 25% for Brazil and between 12% and 18% for Mexico, Argentina,
Philippines and Indonesia. A similar comparative picture emerges when one
looks at the ratios of the relevant stocks (see Table 4.1). Also, DFI in
Korea was confined to relatively few industrial sectors such as chemicals,
electronics and hotels. Sectors with large domestic sales (foodstuffs and
pharmaceuticals, for example) as well as those with established export markets
(textiles for example) did not feature much DFI (see Table 4.2). A further
consequence of Korea's attitude towards DFI was that the forms it took were
largely those in which control often rested with the local partner. Less-
than-majority-owned joint ventures increased relative to majority-owned
ventures during the 1970s. Licensing agreements also grew in importance and
became the preferred form of technology transfer in many sectors.

Table 4.1: SHARES OF DFI IN TOTAL EXTERNAL LIABILITIES

Countries	Stock of DFI, 1983	Stock of external debt, 1983	Ratio of DFI to total liabilities (%)
	-----(billions of US dollars)-----		
Korea	1.8	38.9	4.4
Argentina	5.8	44.4	11.6
Brazil	24.6	88.0	21.8
Mexico	13.6	89.4	13.2
Indonesia	6.8	30.4	18.3
Philippines	2.7	23.9	10.9
Hong Kong	4.2	5.5	43.2
Singapore	7.9	0.7	91.9
Malaysia	6.2	15.9	28.1
Turkey	1.2	17.5	6.4

Source: IMF (1985) and staff calculations.

Table 4.2: VOLUME AND DISTRIBUTION OF DFI /a
(US$ million)

Sector	1972-76	1977-81	1982	1983	1984	1985	Cumulative Total
Agriculture	5.2	6.3.	1.3	1.1	0.6	3.7	19.3
Manufacturing	427.3	223.3	122.3	102.9	264.3	181.9	1574.9
Textiles	57.5	2.5	3.0	1.9	1.9	0.8	72.5
Chemicals	146.1	120.2	41.3	7.6	6.7	44.7	378.4
Machinery	30.3	39.6	9.8	5.7	131.5	50.7	277.5
Electronics	83.0	107.8	19.2	41.4	67.5	55.8	386.2
Services	132.6	188.1	64.2	163.7	154.2	346.2	1060.8
Hotels	10.20	70.5	28.1	155.7	118.4	312.3	713.0
Total	565.2	587.7	187.8	267.8	419.0	531.7	2655

/a On approval basis.

Source: Economic Planning Board.

4.03   Among the reasons often advanced to explain the relative decline of DFI flows to developing countries during the 70's are the shift of world savings to OPEC countries and the availability of bank loans at very low interest rates. It has been argued that the supply of investible funds fell relative to that of loans because OPEC countries, not having technology or management to offer, disposed of their windfall gains in the form of increased bank deposits. These factors may have been important in Korea's case also but were probably of lesser consequence than a number of domestic factors, some beyond and some within policy control. Among the former must be counted Korea's poor endowment of natural extractable resources and problem with national security and political stability. Among the latter must be counted such factors as the reluctance to allow foreign firms to acquire dominant positions in the economy and to benefit from the special incentives offered by Government to promote the manufacturing sector. Since Korea developed its industrial base in considerable measure through special incentives there was an understandable disinclination to see some of those go to foreign firms and eventually become part of their repatriable profits. Furthermore, the industries that were to form the bulk of Korea's manufacturing sector were mostly simple in their technology needs--they required mostly foreign capital and not foreign management expertise. For a variety of reasons, therefore, Korea maintained a generally restrictive and stand-offish attitude towards DFI.[44]

4.04   _Present Policy towards DFI_. Government policy towards DFI experienced a reversal in 1980 when, in an attempt to cope with an economic crisis featuring high inflation, negative growth, growing debt-service difficulties and a large balance of payments deficit, a broad-based program of trade and financial liberalization was adopted. Among the elements of this program were several measures to liberalize the regulations governing DFI.[45] Since then the scope for DFI has generally been expanded and the procedures simplified. In particular, under a set of guidelines adopted in July 1984, an automatic approval system and a negative list system have come into operation which now make Korea one of the more open or least restrictive countries as far as regulations governing DFI are concerned. Only 82 of Korea's 999 industrial sectors are prohibited to foreign investment and a further 215 are subject to strict restrictions. The remaining 660 sectors are now open. Among the

---

44/   Among the strictly economic concerns that DFI has often raised are whether such inflows simply substitute for domestic savings and investment and whether they affect the balance of payments adversely by entailing import-intensive production. A recent study of the effects of foreign direct investment (Shin, 1985) suggests that neither of these concerns are valid for Korea. It finds no statistically significant substitution relationship between domestic and foreign investment nor any adverse effects on the balance of payments during the 1970s. Koo (1984) is of the opinion that the balance of payments impact of DFI has been "positive, substantial and increasing in recent years."

45/   Government's program to liberalize DFI regulations was endorsed in the second Structural Adjustment Loan arranged by the World Bank for Korea in 1983.

522 sectors that are classified as manufacturing about 86% are now open. In the open sectors, a project is given automatic approval if the amount of foreign investment is not more than the equivalent of $1 million and the ratio of foreign investment is less than 50%. In addition to more liberal guidelines for investment and the standard guarantees for repatriation Korea now encourages DFI also through its trade and financial liberalization policies which permit greater flexibility in decisions regarding sourcing of inputs and disposition of outputs, in the use of financial facilities, in the management of liabilities and in foreign exchange dealings. The liberalization program should also enhance Korea's competitiveness and thereby make it even more attractive a haven for DFI.

4.05   The improved environment for DFI since 1980 has shown encouraging results. The amount of DFI approved has increased each year since then and grew to over $500 million in 1985. Up to 1981 the cumulative volume of such investment was around $1.2 billion. Since then the cumulative stock has more than doubled to $2.6 billion (see Table 4.2). Such investment is becoming an important source of funding and technology in several sectors (such as automobiles and electronics) that are now at the leading edge of Korea's drive to attain developed-country status.

B. Future Context of DFI

4.06   Since the 1970's, both the domestic and the international environments have changed and are changing in ways that suggest that a country like Korea would benefit considerably from a future external financing program that emphasizes equity instruments in preference to debt. The international financial environment has changed in several respects. Firstly, because of the considerable adjustment and restructuring that took place in response to high energy costs and inflation during the last decade the OECD corporate sector has reduced costs, increased productivity and strengthened finances, thereby becoming a substantial repository of investible capital. This feature has been significantly bolstered by the substantial drop in the price of oil during 1986. The distribution of world savings is now shifting to the OECD non-financial corporate sector. Secondly, the experience of the debt crisis in the early 1980s has encouraged a preference among investors for marketable instruments as opposed to illiquid instruments.

4.07   The domestic environment has changed substantially also. Korea is now a semi-industrialized country with a sizable pool of strong and savvy domestic entrepreneurs some of whom have built world-class conglomerates. One indication of the growing confidence of Korean entrepreneurs is the substantial number of joint ventures and licensing agreements arranged in recent years at the initiative of Korean producers. The danger that foreign investments might choke nascent domestic enterprise is practically non-existent now. Indeed, where once it was feared that large foreign companies would establish oligopolistic control over the economy, it is now thought that a dose of foreign competition would serve to counteract and reduce oligopolistic domination of the economy by domestic conglomerates.

4.08   The role of government has also been changing such that the promotion of specific industries through special incentives is not expected to be a major factor in future industrial and financial policy and performance. A program of liberalization is under way in accordance with which the variety of incentives provided to the domestic manufacturing sector through trade and credit policies is being reduced. As a result the argument that foreign investors would benefit from special incentives needed only by domestic industry will have less relevance in the future. Furthermore, the program of liberalization will create a market-determined structure of relative prices for domestic and traded goods and factors (e.g. domestic credit, foreign exchange, wage costs) and hence the possibility of multinational firms taking advantage of distorted prices will be minimized. Given a strong indigenous entrepreneur group and given a set of appropriate, market-oriented domestic macroeconomic policies, there is little reason to fear 'exploitation' by foreign investors.

4.09   DFI may also be important to Korea for reasons related to trade diplomacy. Korea now depends heavily on the ability to import technology and capital goods and to export finished and semi-finished manufactures. Should either activity falter, Korea would be affected significantly. There is some fear that, in the future, the sort of technology Korea needs (in automotive and electronics, for example) will not be available "off the shelf" but will come jointly with foreign management and equity. Korea is now moving into areas which require sophisticated advanced technologies which they are unlikely to obtain through old-style licensing agreements. A case in point is video tape recording (VTR) technology which Japanese proprietors are unwilling to part with outside the controlled arrangement of a joint or wholly owned venture.[46]   There is also some fear that the rate of export growth will be severely affected by OECD protectionism. Active trade diplomacy with a view to minimizing the risk of a sharp reduction in technology transfer or in export growth and diversification should have high priority on the Korean strategy agenda. Among the elements of such diplomacy should be a greater emphasis on the potential role of direct foreign investment in offsetting the risk of trade disruptions, in maintaining an inward flow of high technology as well as in relieving the pressure of protectionism in export markets. The larger the stake that OECD corporations have in Korea's industrial growth the better the chances that they will look upon trade disruption with disfavor and will rally with Korea against attempts to restrict trade.

4.10   Finally, as already indicated in earlier sections, equity inflows are advantageous in that they have many desirable characteristics from the perspective of external liability management. With equity inflows project risk is spread, repayments are linked to the ability to pay and a wide range of investors is attracted. Furthermore, since the degree of reinvestment is partly determined by economic policies and incentives provided by the host

---

46/   This unwillingness is rooted in the apprehension that Korean licensees might learn quickly and strike out on their own, thereby threatening Japanese market share in VTRs just as has happened in the case of color TV sets, a product the Koreans learnt to manufacture with the help of licensing agreements with US and Japanese firms.

country, there is a greater possibility of employing DFI flows to aid in the adjustment process in the event of an external shock.

4.11   The Cost of DFI in Korea. One measure of the cost of DFI is the amount of earnings remitted out of the host country or, more usefully, the ratio of dividend remittances to the total stock of DFI. This measure enables a comparison to be made with the cost of incurring debt as measured by the interest rate. Normally one would expect the cost of DFI to be higher than the cost of debt since the foreign investor bears greater risk and has to be compensated for doing so. Thus DFI could involve a greater foreign exchange cost for the host country than debt. However some part or all of the repatriable earnings can be retained and reinvested, an occurrence whose probability increases with the profitability of investing in the country. If a sufficient fraction of such earnings are retained it is quite possible that the foreign exchange cost of servicing the investment, i.e. the ratio of remittances to investment, may be lower than the cost of servicing an equivalent amount of foreign debt. This is clearly an empirical matter. Table 4.3 gives some comparative data for the case of Korea. It appears that in the 1980s Korea has serviced DFI at a lower cost than it has serviced external debt. On average, it has paid almost 10% on its debt but less than 5% as dividend remittances. Even during the 1970's, despite the prevalence of lower interest rates, debt servicing tended to be more expensive than equity servicing for Korea (Koo, 1981). These direct, short-run cost comparisons are, of course, only indicative. Indirect costs or long-term costs may make a difference. For example, the cost of servicing equity may be underestimated in Table 4.3 to the extent that equity investors enjoy capital gains and those may be quite substantial in an inflationary environment. It is, at any rate, possible to claim that DFI does not necessarily impose a larger short-run servicing cost in terms of dividend remittances.

Table 4.3: DIVIDEND REMITTANCE RATES VERSUS INTEREST RATES
(%)

Year	Effective rate of /a interest payment	Effective rate of /b dividend remittance
1974	4.3	5.0
1975	5.8	4.7
1977	6.3	6.8
1979	6.1	5.8
1980	10.9	4.4
1981	12.0	4.2
1982	10.6	4.5
1983	8.7	4.0
1984	9.2	4.5
1985	8.2	6.3

/a   Calculated as ratio of interest payment to average foreign debt outstanding.
/b   Calculated as ratio of remittance to average stock of DFI.

Source: Staff calculations.

Further promotion

4.12   The preceding discussion may be summarized as follows: DFI would appear to hold several advantages for Korea in the present stage of its development: it may be useful from the point of view of liability management, it may be necessary for the transfer of some types of sophisticated technology and it may play a positive role in trade diplomacy. It also appears from the evidence that DFI has not been a comparatively expensive financing option in the past. Some of these considerations, particularly that of the transfer of certain technologies, are reflected in Government's attitude towards DFI as embodied in the Sixth Plan.

4.13   <u>Sixth Plan Targets</u>. Direct foreign investment has been given a more prominent role in the external financing program associated with the Sixth Plan than was the case with previous Plans. The objective of increasing DFI inflows has now become an integral part of the external liability management strategy adopted by Government. Such inflows are expected to grow from around $250 million per annum (on a disbursement basis) at present to $700 million per annum by 1991. Given that the projected external financing requirements will grow at a lower rate than that expected for inflows of DFI, the ratio of DFI to both flows and stocks of external liabilities can be expected to grow. According to projections prepared by the Economic Planning Board, DFI inflows will make up about 11% of total foreign capital inflows (of $6.6 billion) in 1991, up from about 4% currently. It is expected that around 90% of Korea's industries will by then be open to DFI.

4.14   While present regulations and domestic macroeconomic policies provide an appropriate environment for DFI Korea might benefit from some active promotion in Europe so as to broaden the sources of funds, as at present the bulk of DFI in Korea is accounted for by Japanese and US firms. As liberalization progresses it may also be useful to increase the ceiling for investments to qualify for automatic approval. The present ceiling of $1 million may prove to be restrictive for certain types of technology-intensive investments in which other developing countries may also be interested and for which, therefore, speed of approval and low "transaction" costs for the foreign investor may be critical. Indeed the ultimate goal must be to provide parity of treatment across domestic and foreign ventures as far as licensing and approvals are concerned.[47] Parity of treatment should encompass the simultaneous withdrawal of special incentives (e.g. tax exemptions) that apply to DFI but not to domestic ventures together with the elimination of specific disincentives and restrictions.

---

[47] In the future it is quite possible that the limiting factors will not be at the level of macroeconomic policy or general regulations but at the level of the firm. It is possible that DFI will be limited if Korea develops a reputation for labor union problems, joint venture partner problems or discriminatory treatment by bureaucrats. The political climate will also be a relevant determinant.

C. Quasi-Equity Investment

4.15   Since the early 1970s alternatives of foreign direct and foreign portfolio investment have emerged which also provide a link between debt-servicing costs and a project's outcome. These "new forms of investment" (Oman, 1984) aim at "unbundling" the typical direct investment package into its consistent components--for example, capital, technology and control. The objective of the new forms of investment is to permit the host country to single out those features of a project that foreigners have a comparative advantage in supplying and to contract for these features while retaining overall control of the operation. In this way host countries aim to enhance local firms' access to world export markets, to increase the local share of economic rents derivable from extractive industries, to encourage the transfer of "appropriate" technologies, and to increase local entrepreneurship and management skills. The following are the most common new forms of investments: joint ventures, licensing arrangements, franchising, management contracts, production sharing, revenue sharing and profit sharing.[48]

4.16   While the new forms of investment embody the desirable characteristics of capital inflow outlined in Chapter 1 to a significant extent, in two important respects, they may be somewhat less favorable than foreign direct investment: there is some shifting of project risk back to the host economy and the returns on some new forms of investment may be less related to ability to pay. With regard to ability to pay, the returns to the foreign investor

---

48/   A joint venture normally implies the sharing of assets, risks and profits, and participation in the ownership of a particular enterprise. To be considered different from standard DFI the host country should hold at least 50% of the equity. Occasionally, under a "fade-out" agreement, the foreign investor may agree to reduce his share over time. Licensing agreements are contracts under which a foreign investor provides the local licensee with access to technology or know-how most commonly in return for royalties or a percentage of sales or profits. Franchising is a particular type of licensing agreement whereby the local franchise is provided with a package not only of technology and know-how but also local exclusively and management assistance, generally in return for royalties. Management contracts stipulate that a foreign company manage a project or enterprise in the host country. The skills usually provided by the managing firm include knowledge of international product and financial markets and access to funding. A production sharing agreement entitles the lender to a specified proportion of the output of a project in return for an input of capital, technology, marketing and management skills (Lessard, 1985). This form of investment is frequently used in the extractive industries, as an alternative to direct investment. Under revenue sharing and profit sharing arrangements the foreign investor shares respectively in the revenue or profit generated by the project; these forms of investment come progressively closer to full direct investment, since the foreign investor acquires an interest in the outcome of the project but without any share in ownership.

under a number of types of new investment do not depend upon the project's profit performance; for example, royalites are frequently based on the quantity of production or on gross revenue, measures which need not reflect the success of the project (by linking returns directly to outcomes, joint ventures are the exception). In most other respects, the inflow characteristics of the new forms of investment are very similar to those of direct foreign investment. Since both types of investment are project related there is significant risk dispersal within the host economy, the maturities are related to the life of the project, foreign currency exposure does not arise and both types of investment tend to reduce the proportion of capital flows provided by the international banking sector.

4.17   The new forms of investment also have certain disadvantages for the host country. First, they tend to provide incentives for foreign investors to sell plant, equipment and services to developing countries, often financed by bank credits thereby exacerbating debt servicing difficulties. Secondly, the balance-of-payments advantages of the new forms may be less than expected as licensing arrangements are often used by multinational corporations as an alternative means of transfer pricing. Finally, host country control may in practice be quite limited, mainly because of lack of management and technical expertise.

4.18   From the point of view of the foreign investor the new forms of investment offer a number of potential advantages. Where the degree of risk differs across the categories of activity bundled together in traditional direct investment, they permit exploitation of comparative advantage in risk bearing. This unbundling should, therefore, enable the host country to package risk in a manner best suited to various investor groups. For example, licensing and franchising agreements are more likely to appeal to multi-national corporations while revenue and profit sharing might attract support from institutional investors since they are, in effect, project loans with an opportunity to participate in upside potential. In general, foreign investors see the new forms of investment as means of minimizing project risk while a the same time maximizing the leverage of the capital invested.

4.19   Application to Korea. Two new forms of investment dominate in Korea--joint ventures and licensing agreements. The number of less-than-majority-foreign owned joint ventures is significant and has increased relative to wholly-owned and majority-owned firms. Licensing agreements, especially by local firms and joint ventures, have also been important and their number has grown faster than investments in majority-wholly-owned-foreign firms (Koo, 1984). The trend, particularly since the early 1970s, has been one of a noticeable increase in the importance of these two new forms relative to traditional direct investment.

4.20   Korea's rapid technological advance during the 1960s and 1970s has been cited in support of the hypothesis that new forms of investment offer important advantages over traditional foreign direct investment in the area of technology transfer and the development of local technological capacity (Oman, 1984). The argument is that once in possession of this technology Korean firms would be in a position to challenge for export markets worldwide whereas under the traditional forms of investment the output of Korean firms would in certain circumstances be determined by the foreign investor. On the basis of licensing agreements Korea was in fact able to acquire the most sophisticated technology including that in the shipbuilding and steel industries. Korea's export-led industrialization has overwhelmingly been directed and controlled by nationals who have relied heavily on indigenous effort through various forms of learning-by-doing and an emphasis on arm's length transactions in the use of foreign resources. Thus, the new forms of investment seem more appropriate for a country like Korea which is in the latter stages of industrialization.

4.21   From the point of view of the desirable inflow characteristics, there is little to choose between investment in the form of venture capital and licensing agreements on the one hand and traditional direct investment on the other, although the latter may have a somewhat better ability to pay and risk sharing features. By comparison with general obligation finance all three types of investment perform very satisfactorily. However, the new forms of investment may be preferred when account is taken of the Korean preference for limited foreign ownership of domestic firms, of the ability of local entrepreneurs to exploit the opportunities presented by the new forms of investment and of the likelihood that capital inflows in this form would be more suitable to Korea's present phase of economic development. While the choice between the various new forms of investment would be mainly based on industrial policy considerations, from the narrow point of view of debt management preference should probably be given to joint ventures over licensing agreements because of their superior ability-to-pay feature. None of the other new forms of investment seem particularly relevant to Korea.

V. ELEMENTS OF A DESIRABLE FINANCING STRATEGY FOR KOREA

A. Assessment of Instruments

5.01   The preceding chapters (and appendices) have discussed, inter alia, desirable external financing objectives for Korea and the extent to which various conventional and innovative international capital market instruments might be suitable for Korea. Since a large number of instruments has been covered it may be useful to review their properties in the form of a matrix (see Table 5.1) which cross-classifies instruments by desirable inflow characteristics.

5.02   There are considerable differences in the extent to which the various instruments embody the desirable inflow characteristics. Indeed, the gap between the ranking of direct investment and the various types of portfolio investment on the one hand and general obligation finance on the other is quite striking, clearly illustrating the disadvantages of the latter type of finance for developing countries. The high score of the former instruments reflects the fact that they do not give rise to currency exposure, their maturities are related to the life of the project, debt service depends on project success while risk is effectively shifted to the foreign investor and not to the host government. Moreover, these forms of investment would diversify the sources of external finance away from international banks and would also be in a form that would facilitate the attainment of macroeconomic objectives in Korea. The other instruments included in the table embody the desirable characteristics to a greater or a lesser degree. The next highest ranking group of instruments are the new forms of investment which are also project and enterprise specific. The differences between the new forms of investment and direct/portfolio investment are not significant: some licensing arrangements have the disadvantage that, if the return is in the form of royalties, it may not be related to project profitability while, in the case of joint ventures, there is some shifting of project risk back to the host country.

5.03   Instruments that increase the flexibility of debt service obligations tend to score surprisingly well given that they all take the form of loans. In the case of graduated payment loans and shared equity loans this high score is partly explained by the fact that debt service under these instruments is related to project success while the extended maturity feature of variable maturity loans is particularly attractive. Moreover, since all three types of loan can be used for project financing they would tend to promote risk dispersal in the economy. Also, if such loans were successfully contracted, they would of necessity tend to diversify the sources of Korean borrowing. However, as indicated in Chapter 2, it is unlikely that such innovations in the area of syndicated credits will be available to Korea on financially attractive terms in the immediate future.

Table 5.1: CLASSIFICATION OF INSTRUMENTS BY INFLOW CHARACTERISTICS

Instruments	Longer maturities	Diversified currencies	Risk sharing	Risk dispersal	Correlation with ability to pay	Diversity of sources
Portfolio Investment	H	H	H	H	H	H
Direct Investment	H	H	H	H	H	H
New Forms of Investment						
Licensing agreements	H	H	M	H	M	H
Joint ventures	H	H	M	H	H	H
Smooth Real Debt Service						
Index-linked bond	M	M	L	L	M	H
Constant debt service FRN	M	M	L	L	M	M
Risk Shifting						
Commodity bonds	M	M	H	L	H	H
Trade bonds	M	M	H	L	H	H
Increased Flexibility						
Flexible maturity loan	H	M	L	H	M	H
Graduated payment loan	M	M	M	H	H	H
Shared equity loan	M	M	M	H	H	H
Non-Recourse Financing	M	L	H	H	H	L
General Obligation Finance						
Standard Loans	L	M	L	L	L	L
Standard Bonds	M	M	L	L	L	M

Code: Extent to which instruments embody desirable characteristics: L = little M = Moderately; H = to a large extent.

5.04   Potential instruments that shift risk such as commodity and trade bonds also rank relatively highly. The major differences between these instruments and other risk-shifting instruments (such as direct and portfolio investment) is that the former would appear to require a government guarantee, as well as the fact their maturity and currency characteristics may be somewhat less favorable. Nevertheless, from the borrowers' perspective, these instruments have many attractions.

5.05   Non-recourse financing and instruments that smooth real debt service payments rank lower (although even these would represent a marked improvement over general obligation finance). Rather poor risk sharing and risk dispersal features together with the fact that although real debt service has a smooth time profile it is not related to ability to pay, reduce somewhat the benefits of index-linked bonds and constant debt payment FRNs. Non-recourse financing scores highly on risk dispersal and transfer but less so on the ability to pay, currency and diversity-of-sources characteristics, in which respects it resembles general obligation financing.

5.06   Financing Constraints and Opportunities. A logical conclusion to be drawn from the preceding discussion is that, from the borrowers' point of view, the composition of capital inflows should be largely in the form of direct and portfolio investment, new forms of investment and trade bonds and, to a lesser extent, instruments that increase repayment flexibility and non-recourse loans. As a financing strategy, however, this approach would not be realistic. This is so first because it pays little regard to the existing pattern of capital inflows into Korea; secondly, because it ignores investors' preferences as revealed in the trend to securitization and thirdly, because some of the instruments are new to international financing and may not be available to Korea at financially attractive and competitive terms.

5.07   The share of syndicated bank loans in Korean inflows of medium- and long-term capital has declined from around 90% in the late 70's to about 55% in recent years. Over the same period bond issues increased sharply to about 30% of total inflows. Direct investment and portfolio investment between them however, still account for less than 5% of such inflows. In view of these shares and the trends behind them it would be unrealistic to expect a rapid shift away from reliance on general obligation finance although much could be done within this category of finance. This observation has consequences for a future strategy for external financing: in the short-run efforts should be concentrated on adjusting the existing array of instruments to bring them more into line with the desirable inflow characteristics; in the longer run, however, it should be recognized that the existing structure is not immutable and a strategy aimed at promoting greater use of equity instruments is both possible and desirable.

5.08   As well as satisfying borrowers' requirements, instruments designed to improve the composition of developing countries' capital inflow should be consistent with investors' preferences and in particular with the trend towards securitization in international capital markets. This trend towards securitization involves a shift in credit flows from bank lending to market-able debt instruments and has manifested itself in both a sharp increase in the share of international credit in the form of securitized assets as well as

in the development, within the syndicated loan market, of instruments that
increase the negotiability of traditional bank assets. The rise in the relative importance of bond markets has reflected the absence of debt-servicing
difficulties in these markets and the fact that it has become cheaper for
prime non-bank borrowers to raise funds through these markets than from
banks. The securitization trend implies that Korea should look more to the
note and bond markets and less to syndicated loan arrangements for future
finance as indeed it has been doing in recent years.

5.09   Another aspect of the recent rapid innovation in international
credit markets is the blurring of the distinction between bond and equity markets. The vast amount of convertible bonds issued over the last decade has
served to condition investors to view bonds and equities as part of a spectrum
of investment instruments rather than as two separate markets. This development has stimulated the development of hybrid securities which allow investors
to receive dividends or participate in profits without putting them under the
same obligations or permitting them the same rights as ordinary shareholders. Such arrangements have the advantage of not undermining the existing
ownership structure of a company and have proved to be very popular with
investors. The growing preference for equity related debt suggests that Korea
should explore this market segment to a greater extent in the future.

B.   Short-Term Debt Strategy for Korea

5.10   The discussion in Chapter 2 has indicated that Korea has
historically had few degrees of freedom to maneuver in international capital
markets: it has not had access to fixed rate US dollar or Eurodollar facilities, the secondary market in its bonds is illiquid, its paper is narrowly
held, it has had only limited opportunities to avail of long-term maturities
and some of its traditional bankers have been reducing their exposures
recently.

5.11   Recent developments in the international trade and finance arena,
however, provide grounds for considerable optimism with regard to Korea's
future external financing situation.[49] It would appear from these developments that, in the foreseeable near term, the available supply of external
funds will exceed the demand for such finance by Korea and, as a consequence,
the terms and conditions attached to future financing arrangements will move
in Korea's favor. More importantly, the near future offers an excellent

---

[49] These favorable developments are principally the substantial decline in
the price of oil and in international interest rates and the sharp appreciation of the Japanese yen relative to the Korean won. Should the current alignment of prices be sustained, it is extremely likely that Korea
will move into a balance of payments surplus situation (of $4 billion in
1986 and to $3 billion per annum and beyond). Its external financing
requirements will thus be substantially reduced for the medium term (from
$6.8 billion in 1985 to $1.6 billion in 1986 and $6.5 billion per annum
(on average) during 1987-91, according to EPB projections) despite rising
amortizations.

opportunity for Korea to modify its external liability structure in more desirable directions.

5.12   The Supply of External Finance. The oil price drop of recent months has, apart from reducing Korea's need for external finance, led to two developments which have increased the potential availability or supply of such finance to Korea. First, it has boosted the OECD's financial surplus and second it has forced such oil dependent countries as Indonesia and Malaysia to reduce their expenditures, thereby reducing the demand for external finance among East Asian developing countries. Thus, 1986 should see a large OECD (but mostly Japanese) financial surplus chasing dwindling lending opportunities in East Asia.

5.13   These developments are likely to have two consequences for Korea. First, its spreads should decline since Korea now presents one of the few good lending opportunities to foreign bankers in their East Asian operations. Some evidence of this its already available. Spreads on syndicated credits for Korea have declined compared to 1985. For example, Korea Exchange Bank (KEB) arranged a $375 million dollar loan in March 1986 which was structured as follows: two years at 0.5% and six years at 0.625% above LIBOR respectively. This compares with a KEB loan for $400 million dollars in March 1985 which was structured as three years at 0.625% and five years at 0.75% above LIBOR respectively. It is thought that spreads will decline even more towards the end of the year as the demand for funds by traditional East Asian borrowers continues to slacken.

5.14   A second consequence of recent developments is that more and more of Korea's external funding is likely to come from Japan. In the first instance, among OECD countries Japan has been the major beneficiary of the oil price drop. This windfall has added to its already huge trade surplus. In the second instance, Japanese financial institutions have better knowledge of the Korean market than their European counterparts. Thirdly, the previously dominant US banks have been reducing their exposures to Korea for the past three years for reasons related to their changing global strategies and changing capital-asset regulations in the wake of the Latin debt crisis. For all these reasons, it seems likely that much of the new external financing business in Korea, be it loans or bonds, will be taken up by the Japanese. It is thought that they picked up 70% of the net increase in Korean exposure in 1985 and may pick up a higher share in 1986. Indeed, they have been most aggressive in competing for Korean business this year by softening terms ahead of and more than their competitors.[50]

5.15   Korea should be able to take advantage of the external finance enviroment it faces currently not only to reduce the average cost of its financing but also to improve the structure of its liabilities. Indeed it is precisely in such a "borrowers-market" situation that the scope for borrower innovation is greatest. Some of the steps that Korea might consider are discussed below.

Possible Actions in the Loan and Bond Markets

5.16   _Maturity_: It has been noted in (in Chapter 1) that while Korea has made much progress in reducing the proportion of short-term debt in its total liabilities there is room for improvement in the medium- and long-term category. In general, longer maturities are more expensive for the borrower but, under present market circumstances, the increase in cost should be minimal. Given the lack of alternative opportunities in the East Asian region for banks and other investors, and given Korea's excellent economic prospects, investors should be willing to provide 15 to 25 year maturities to Korea. It is important for Korea to establish a precedent since once a precedent is set in obtaining a loan or floating a bond of a certain maturity the market generally finds it easier to accept "repeaters" on the same or better terms. In order to set such a precedent Korea must forgo a part of the reduction in spreads that it can expect under present market conditions but it should be willing to do so since the relative price of extra years of maturity in terms of spread points is currently very favorable.[51] It might also be noted that it is far more likely that such maturities will be available for FRN's than for conventional syndicated credits. Furthermore, even with FRN's, the longer maturities cannot be obtained straight away. Korea may have to build towards them in stages, by first issuing say a 15 year note successfully and then following it up at reasonable intervals by issues of 20 year and 25 year maturities.

50/ Discussions with the Japanese financial community suggest additional reasons why the Japanese appetite for foreign business is likely to grow. A process of financial deregulation is underway in Japan which involves some relaxation of the regulations governing foreign lending and investing. Furthermore, the number of institutions that are involved in foreign lending is also growing--insurance companies, leasing companies, regional banks, and securities houses are increasingly encroaching upon the preserve that was once largely that of the major Japanese commercial banks.

51/ Obtaining longer maturities should also be facilitated by the fact that the capacity of large Japanese commercial banks to undertake long-term lending has recently grown because of deregulation in Japan which has increased these banks' ability to raise long-term funds from domestic sources.

5.17   Swaps: Korea should also conintue altering the currency and
interest-type mix of its liabilities through the use of swaps. For example,
as already noted, Korea has virtually no direct access to fixed-rate US or
Eurodollar facilities but has excellent access to fixed and floating rate yen
facilities. It should consider trading on its comparative advantage and swap
some of its floating rate yen or dollar liabilities into fixed rate dollar
ones. Of course, the timing of the swap should be carefully considered since
terms and conditions vary from day to day. What is being recommended here is
that an active currency management strategy be adopted as a part of the overall debt management program.

5.18   Coordination: In the syndicated loan market, there would appear to
be a continuous stream of Korean syndications: some streamlining of these
borrowings would appear to be desirable. The 'sovereign' borrowers also fail
to diversify their funding requirements or to segment the international banking market. This strategy enables banks to 'hold-the-line' on spreads, reference rates and other charges on Korean facilities. A more effective strategy
might involve seeking proposals from lead banks which would be specially targeted at different segments of the banking market: this would enable Korea to
benefit from the competition being provided at present by Japanese banks.
This would require significant coordination of the three 'sovereign'
borrowers' activities in the syndicated-loan market. An alternative market-
segmentation strategy would be to approach the bond market rather than the
bank loan market. Since this market has more participants it is less
oligopolistic and less subject to rate fixing maneuvers. By developing a
significant alternative source of funds via the bond market Korea can also put
pressure on its syndicated credit suppliers to reduce their spreads, fees and
other charges.

5.19   Prepayment: In view of the decline in international interest rates
and spreads, the greatest benefit to Korea, in terms of cost savings, would
come from the replacement of existing loans with facilities reflecting
existing market conditions. Korea's current attempts to prepay some existing
loans and to refinance some others at more favorable terms can, therefore, be
understood. The only note of caution one might sound here is that the option
of prepayment and/or refinancing should be carefully evaluated so as not to
impair existing relationships with traditional lenders. However, considering
the extent of similar renegotiations that have been conducted recently,
especially by sovereign borrowers, Korea's attempts to benefit from existing
market conditions should not damage its access to international financial
markets.

5.20   Private versus Public Debt: The sharp improvement in Korea's economic prospects occasioned by the decline in the price of oil and the appreciation of the yen relative to the won heralds new opportunities for Korea in international capital markets. Korea now anticipates sizable balance of payments surpluses over the near future and its major private corporations are
now in a position to establish significant market shares and brand-name presence in OECD markets. As a result the need for public or semi-public borrowing for balance of payments purposes is declining while the prospects of

Korean corporations being able to borrow in their own names, and without government-guarantees, are improving. The opportunity exists, therefore, for Korea to encourage a shift from public foreign debt towards private non-guaranteed debt. This would have the benefits of dispersing default-risk away from the Government and increasing the familiarity of Korean corporate names in international capital markets. Towards this end Government should encourage private borrowers to adopt financial management, accounting and disclosure practices that will help them in converting their bright economic prospects into enhanced access to external finance. Any marketing effort undertaken to promote the semi-public names can also have positive spillover effects for private Korean corporate names. The recent assignment of favorable credit ratings to Korean sovereign risk by Moodys and S&P's also bodes well for private Korean names although the advantage is more likely to be perceived in short and medium term financing arrangements than in access to long-term funds.

5.21   Bond Market Strategy: Korea will continue to need to undertake a certain amount of public borrowing in the future in order to refinance some of its existing debt (amortizations are projected at between $4 and $5 billion per annum over the next five years). It may also need to borrow if its balance of payments situation deteriorates on account of exogenous shocks such as increases in oil prices and interest rates or sharp declines in OECD growth rates. While the prospects of significant deterioration in the balance of payments are dim it would nevertheless be prudent to develop a public borrowing strategy that improves on past experience. As part of this strategy, debt securities such as FRN's should be pursued in preference to syndicated credits over the near future because, if approached appropriately, these instruments offer greater scope for reducing costs, lengthening maturities, increasing diversification of funding sources and incorporating borrower-driven innovations.[52] Investors prefer bonds to loans because of the relatively greater liquidity offered by bonds. To obtain liquidity they are prepared to accept finer spreads than they would in the case of loans. Korean bonds, however, have proved not to be very liquid partly because of the Korean practice of coming to the market many times with small issues rather than coming fewer times but with larger issues. Dealers in the secondary market need to maintain inventories of each issue in order to effectively make markets in these issues. There are, however, considerable economies of scale in the holding of inventories, which tend to raise the costs of secondary market trading in small issues and thus impair liquidity. This in turn

---

[52] This is not to say that syndicated credits should be abandoned. There is one very good reason why even comfortably off borrowers should not damage their links with traditional bank lenders: times can change and banks can be useful on 'rainy days'. In Korea's case, however, it would appear that the existing amount of business in the form of syndicated credits is so large that even a substantial reduction should not affect its long term relationships with its bankers. Indeed some reduction in business would permit the rebuilding of "credit reserves" with many traditional lenders and lessen the pressure on exposure limits that has been worrying them in recent years.

implies that Korean issues typically carry a yield premium to compensate for the lack of liquidity.[53] In this context, it is also worth noting that the size of swap-related issues needs to be quite large in order to make the swap worthwhile to all participants.

5.22   It is possible that the public sector banking institutions suffer to some extent from the general perception that Korea's financial sector is weak and underdeveloped and from the lack of awareness of Korean 'names' in most capital markets. If this is the case, then Korea may be paying more for not borrowing in its own name. The differential terms obtained at times in both the syndicated loan and FRN markets by Korea's 'benchmark borrowers' also tend to support this proposition. While it is difficult to be definite on this issue, on balance the evidence would seem to suggest that Korea would benefit from a switch to 'full' sovereign borrowing.

5.23   A bond market strategy that would stand the best chance of overcoming the present perception of Korean paper would need to combine the following elements: (a) the size of issue should be large, say a minimum of $250 million, so as to generate liquidity;[54] (b) the issues should be in government name so as not to be compared with the past history of Korean FRN's associated with the 'semi-sovereign' borrowers; government name is most likely to insure a longer maturity and generally better terms as well as to attract a wider investor base; and (c) care should be taken to ensure that lead managers are chosen for their non-bank placement capabilities so as to reduce debt-concentration in banks.

53/   Another reason advanced for the poor experience of Korean bonds is political risk. Political risk is considered to be high for Korea because of its security problems. This makes it difficult to attract non-bank investors to Korean paper since such investors have poorer knowledge of country details and tend to react more strongly than banks to adverse political news and rumors. The greater the perceived political risk, the more likely it is that Korea's external financing needs will be met by large international banks who have a history of lending to Korea, and the more likely it becomes that such financing will be in the form of syndicated credits rather than bonds.

54/   On the matter of size of issue the following points should also be noted: (a) In some markets there is a 'standard' size of issue set by custom or precedent while in other markets the size of issue is regulated by the monetary authorities; for example, in Japan "samurai" issues are limited to a maximum of Y 30 billion for issuers with a double A rating. (b) If financing needs are limited and diversification across markets is a priority then there may exist a tradeoff between size of issue and diversification; because more markets have to be tapped each market must be approached with a smaller issue than if the total financing needs were to be met from one market.

5.24   Marketing: There also is potential for reducing the concentration
of bond-holding in banks and reliance on floating rate funding. The greatest
potential would initially appear to be in the Japanese market, but the
European, especially the Swiss, markets also warrant further consideration.[55]
In this respect, it might be worth considering a major marketing effort to
attract European fund managers' interest and overcome their lack of familiarity with the Korean situation. Current market circumstances are favorable
for the initiation of a major marketing effort by Korea.

5.25   Euronotes and Commercial Paper: The Euronote market also has
potential for reducing spreads and attracting non-bank investors. Since
corporations are both borrowers and lenders in this market, Korea's
conglomerates may be able to attract the type of investor that would be more
familiar with them. In addition to the Euronote market the US commercial
paper market offers great potential for diversification. Access to both
markets should be enhanced through the acquisition of a US credit rating.

5.26   Convertible Debentures: Advantage should be taken of the current
market preference for hybrid securities in general and the strong interest in
Korean convertible debentures in particular. The three issues floated so far
have met with an enthusiastic response despite their carrying terms which were
very favorable to be issuers. Further issues should be encouraged and the
program of equity market liberalization in this particular regard should be
accelerated to take advantage of market conditions. Bonds with equity
warrants attached are also an attractive possibility. Since Korean equities
are in high demand it would be smart to include them in bond packages in such
a way as to benefit from that demand.

C. Composition of Inflows in Medium- and Long-Term

5.27   The question now arises as to the most appropriate composition of
capital inflows for Korea in the medium and long-term. The scope for improving the terms of bank lending to developing countries to bring them more into
line with the identified desirable characteristics is quite limited, essentially because banks have liabilities that are fixed in money terms and are,
therefore, constrained to seek assets with a similar property. The more
fundamental departures from the traditional forms of lending to developing
countries that would be required to incorporate these characteristics are far
more likely to develop in the capital markets and in direct participation by
multinational companies. Participants in these markets include a wide array
of institutions most of which do not face the accounting constraints on
accepting more innovative assets that the banks do.

55/ The Swiss are widely known for their placing power given the sheer weight
and number of their private customers. As the Economist (September 6,
1986) notes, "Choosing a Swiss bond issue is like choosing a new Mercedes
rather than an old Ford; it may cost more but you are sure of getting to
where you want to be."

5.28   Many of the instruments listed in Table 5.1 would be consistent with trends in international capital markets. Index-linked bonds, constant debt service FRNs, trade and commodity bonds and, of course, portfolio investment are all securitized instruments.[56/] However, the three loan instruments considered - variable maturity loans, graduated payment loans and shared equity loans - could not be regarded as marketable assets (unless loans under the latter instrument could be converted into shares, in which case they would be equivalent to convertible bonds). Moreover, the indefinite maturity feature of the flexible maturity loan and the uncertainty with regard to the timing of amortization under the graduated payment loan would render both these instruments unattractive to banks and possibly less attractive to other institutional investors as well. Thus, having considered at some length the most desirable financing options for Korea from the borrower's point of view and (more briefly) from the lenders' perspective, it might be concluded that index-linked bonds and particularly trade bonds are the only new instruments likely to prove acceptable to both parties.

5.29   Korea should, in the medium to long term, aim to increase substantially the share of capital inflows in the form of equity investment. New types of instruments identified as being suitable for Korea--especially trade bonds--should also be explored keeping in mind, of course, that such bonds have never been issued and considerable technical hurdles may need to be crossed.

5.30   There are numerous reasons for recommending such a strategy. First, the high share of exports in GDP makes Korea exceptionally vulnerable to external shocks and suggests that a high priority should be attached to risk minimization by way of relating debt service to ability to pay. Secondly, Korea's large gross financing requirements up to the end of the decade means that it has a continuing need for secure and significant sources of funds over this period. And, thirdly, the development of private sector mechanisms to spread business risk is essential given that the guarantee of Government "bailouts" can no longer be taken for granted (in accordance with the professed intentions of the Government). The matching of these considerations with the securitization trends in international financial markets including the tendency for a growing share of savings in industrial countries to be directed to non-bank financial institutions suggests that Korea should aim to tap the broader international markets for its medium-term needs. Moreover, with the growing integration of bond and equity markets worldwide, investment managers are tending to look beyond the major industrial countries for invest- ment outlets and Korea with its buoyant export growth and industrial structure comprising large privately-owned firms, has a head start on most developing countries. Thus, Korea would be well placed to capture a major share of any trend towards equity investment in developing countries. A strategy of

---

56/   It may also be noted that the approach represented by the various new forms of investment corresponds with the "unbundling" of risks in financial markets as evidenced by the recent tendency for separate pricing of the interest, liquidity and maturity features of financial instruments.

concentrating on project specific financing should be quite feasible for Korea given that its fiscal deficit is relatively modest, thereby reducing its need for general purpose finance.

5.31   In keeping with this goal Government should strongly consider expanding the existing investment trusts for foreigners to purchase Korean stocks and establishing additional funds, similar to the Korea Fund, on other foreign stock exchanges. Such measures will increase the familiarity of world capital markets with Korean equities and can be implemented quickly. The extent of foreign control of local companies could be limited by the issuing of non-voting shares such as those available in various European countries. Over the longer run the success of a strategy of relying to an increasing extent on portfolio investment will require improvements in the functioning of the domestic capital market and in corporate accounting and disclosure practices. The development and implementation of measures to bring about such improvements will take time and should be taken up as soon as possible. Otherwise there exists the possibility that the enthusiasm with which foreign portfolio investors are greeting various stages of the market-opening program will fizzle out once the market is technically open. To maintain interest and dynamism after that point it will be necessary to attend to the various technical, fiscal, institutional and market development measures already listed.[58]

5.32   There is also a place for the new types of instruments identified as having characteristics particularly useful for Korea--index-linked bonds and especially trade bonds. With the reduction in inflation index-linked bonds may be less relevant today; they are, nevertheless, a useful weapon to have in the armoury in the event of a resurgence of world inflation. The trade bond has an especially attractive feature for Korea: it represents a means of securitizing the performance of the economy as a whole and in this way is fully consistent with recent trends in international financial markets. As yet this instrument has not been issued on financial markets. Moreover, financial innovations of this type would normally be accepted by financial markets only if first issued by prime borrowers. However, if the considerable technical difficulties with these bonds could be overcome the favorable implications of recent oil price developments for Korean economic growth and for Korean exports would increase the attractiveness of Korean trade bonds for foreign investors. Although the combination of a government guarantee and likely high returns to investors might seem overgenerous, this would be balanced by the fact that debt service would be directly related to export earnings.

5.33   Risks and Safeguards. Mention has already been made of the risks associated with lifting restrictions on capital movements in and out of Korea in order to facilitate foreign direct and portfolio investment (see paras. 1.36-1.40). It is worth re-emphasizing here that the risk of macroeconomic instability arising from the possibility of large and volatile capital flows is limited in Korea's case by the fact that such liberalization of capital

---

[58] For details see Chapter 3 and Appendix 3A.

movements as will be necessary will be occurring in a very strong macro-economic context featuring a modest fiscal deficit, a strong current account, an undistorted exchange rate, low inflation and a tradition of economic policy-making of high calibre and credibility. Thus the best way for Korea to contain the possible risk of macroeconomic instability would be to maintain the economic policy regime it has in place currently. Moreover, complete or immediate liberalization of the capital account will not be necessary to attract greater amounts of equity inflows--partial and selective liberalization should suffice. At the same time, monitoring of "large" capital movements should be continued.[59] Finally, the risk of losing control over domestic assets through portfolio foreign investment can be removed by restricting such investment to a class of non-voting shares or by imposing percentage ceilings by firm or industry.

5.36   In summary, a major theme of this report has been that capital inflows to Korea should increasingly be in the form of equity investment. Such a strategy would seek to tap and package the dynamism of the Korean economy in a way that would appeal to a wide range of foreign investors and would be consistent with the recent trend towards securitization in international financial markets. In this way Korea would take a positive step towards the model of financing dominant in the industrial world, a world which on the basis of many economic fundamentals it is ready to join.

---

[59]   The matter of permitting Korean nationals to acquire foreign financial assets (fourth stage of capital market liberalization program) falls outside the scope of this report. At any rate that stage is at least five years away and considerable experience with capital market liberalization will have been gained by then to allow an informed decision to be made.

REFERENCES CITED

ANCKONIE, A. and C.H. Chi, 1986. "Internationalization of the Korean Stock Market" mimeo, Dept. of Business Administration, George Washington University, Washington D.C.

BARTH, Michael and Peter Wall, "The Importance of Portfolio Investment as a Source of Development Finance," mimeo, International Finance Corporation, June 1985.

BRONTE, Stephen, Japanese Finance: Markets and Institutions, Euromoney Publications Ltd., 1982.

GILL, David, "Enhancing Access to Foreign Capital Markets: An Overview: IFC paper delivered to International Conference on Convertible Bonds and International Depository Receipts," Seoul, Korea, September 1985.

GOODMAN, Laurie S. 1982. "An Alternative to Rescheduling LDC Debt in an Inflationary Environment". Columbia Journal of World Business, 17 (Spring).

INTERNATIONAL MONETARY FUND. 1985. Foreign Private Investment in Developing Countries. Occasional Paper No. 33, Washington, DC.

KALDEREN, Lars. 1985. "Techniques of External Debt Management" in Mehran, H. (Ed.) External Debt Management. International Monetary Fund. Washington, D.C.

KOO, B.Y. 1981. "Role of Foreign Direct Investment in Recent Korean Economic Growth" Working Paper No. 8104, Korean Development Institute, Seoul, Korea.

KOO, B.Y. 1982. "New Forms of Foreign Investment in Korea." in Oman (ed), New Forms of Foreign Investment in Developing Countries, Paris: OECD Development Center.

KYLE, S. Essays on the Market Value of Developing Country Debt, Unpublished Ph.D. Dissertation, Harvard University, October 1985.

LESSARD, Donald R. 1977. "Risk Efficient External Financing for Commodity Exporting Countries". Cuadernos de Economics, May.

LESSARD, Donald R. 1985. International Financing for Developing Countries: The Unfulfilled Promise. World Bank Staff Working Paper #792, World Bank, Washington, D.C.

LESSARD, Donald R. and John Williamson. 1985. Financial Intermediation Beyond the Debt Crisis. Policy Analysis in International Economics 12. Washington D.C. Institute for International Economics.

MORGAN GUARANTY. 1984. World Financial Markets, August.

McDONALD, Donough. 1982. "Debt Capacity and Developing Country Borrowing: A Survey of the Literature". _IMF Staff Papers_, Vol. 29, No. 4, December.

MORROW, Barbara, "Issues in the Development of Korean Securities Markets," mimeo, International Finance Corporation, July 1984.

OECD. 1986. _Financial Market Trends_, March.

OMAN, Charles. 1984. _New Forms of International Investment in Developing Countries_. Paris: OECD.

SAINI, Krishnan G. 1986. _Capital Market Innovations and Financial Flows to Developing Countries_. World Bank Staff Working Papers, Number 784.

SHIN, S.D., "The Determinants and Effects of Foreign Direct Investment in Korea," _Quarterly Economic Review_, June 1985, Bank of Korea.

WILLIAMSON, John. 1981. "The Why and How of Funding LDC Debt"; paper presented at the Second Inter-American Conference on Capital Markets, Caracas, Venezuela.

WORLD BANK. 1985. _World Development Report 1985_. Washington, D.C.

WORLD BANK. 1986. _Korea: Managing the Industrial Transition_, Report No. KO-6138, Washington, D.C.

DISTRIBUTORS OF WORLD BANK PUBLICATIONS

ARGENTINA
Carlos Hirsch, SRL
Galeria Guemes
Florida 165, 4th Floor-Ofc. 453/465
1333 Buenos Aires

AUSTRALIA, PAPUA NEW GUINEA, FIJI, SOLOMON ISLANDS, AND VANUATU
Info-Line
Overseas Document Delivery
Box 506, GPO
Sydney, NSW 2001

AUSTRIA
Gerold and Co.
A-1011 Wien
Graben 31

BAHRAIN
MEMRB Information Services
P.O. Box 2750
Manama Town 317

BANGLADESH
Micro Industries Development Assistance Society (MIDAS)
G.P.O. Box 800
Dhaka

BELGIUM
Publications des Nations Unies
Av. du Roi 202
1060 Brussels

BRAZIL
Publicacoes Tecnicas Internacionais Ltda.
Rua Peixoto Gomide, 209
01409 Sao Paulo, SP

CANADA
Le Diffuseur
C.P. 85, 1501 Ampere Street
Boucherville, Quebec
J4B 5E6

CHILE
Editorial Renacimiento
Miraflores 354
Santiago

COLOMBIA
Enlace Ltda.
Carrera 6 No. 51-21
Bogota D.E.
Apartado Aereo 4430
Cali, Valle

COSTA RICA
Libreria Trejos
Calle 11-13
Av. Fernandez Guell
San Jose

COTE D'IVOIRE
Centre d'Edition et de Diffusion Africaines (CEDA)
04 B.P. 541
Abidjan 04 Plateau

CYPRUS
MEMRB Information Services
P.O. Box 2098
Nicosia

DENMARK
SamfundsLitteratur
Rosenoerns Alle 11
DK-1970 Frederiksberg C.

DOMINICAN REPUBLIC
Editora Taller, C. por A.
Restauracion
Apdo. postal 2190
Santo Domingo

EGYPT, ARAB REPUBLIC OF
Al Ahram
Al Galaa Street
Cairo

FINLAND
Akateeminen Kirjakauppa
P.O. Box 128
SF-00101
Helsinki 10

FRANCE
World Bank Publications
66, avenue d'Iena
75116 Paris

GERMANY, FEDERAL REPUBLIC OF
UNO-Verlag
Poppelsdorfer Alle 55
D-5300 Bonn 1

GREECE
KEME
24, Ippodamou Street
Athens-11635

GUATEMALA
Librerias Piedra Santa
Centro Cultural Piedra Santa
11 calle 6-50 zona 1
Guatemala City

HONG KONG, MACAU
Asia 2000 Ltd.
6 Fl., 146 Prince Edward Road, W,
Kowloon
Hong Kong

HUNGARY
Kultura
P.O. Box 139
1389 Budapest 62

INDIA
For single titles
UBS Publishers' Distributors Ltd.
Post Box 7015
New Delhi 110002

10 First Main Road
Gandhi Nagar
Bangalore 560009

Apeejay Chambers, P.O. Box 736
5 Wallace Street
Bombay 400001

8/1-B, Chowringhee Lane
Calcutta 700016

7/188, 1(A), Swarup Nagar
Kanpur 208001

Sivaganga Road
Nungambakkam
Madras 600034

5-A, Rajendra Nagar
Patna 800016

For subscription orders
Universal Subscription Agency Pvt. Ltd.
18-19 Community Centre Saket
New Delhi 110 017

INDONESIA
Pt. Indira Limited
Jl. Sam Ratulangi 37
Jakarta Pusat
P.O. Box 181

IRELAND
TDC Publishers
12 North Frederick Street
Dublin 1

ISRAEL
The Jerusalem Post
The Jerusalem Post Building
P.O. Box 81
Romema Jerusalem 91000

ITALY
Licosa Commissionaria Sansoni SPA
Via Lamarmora 45
Casella Postale 552
50121 Florence

JAPAN
Eastern Book Service
37-3, Hongo 3-Chome, Bunkyo-ku 113
Tokyo

JORDAN
Jordan Center for Marketing Research
P.O. Box 3143
Jabal
Amman

KENYA
Africa Book Service (E.A.) Ltd.
P. O. Box 45245
Nairobi

KOREA, REPUBLIC OF
Pan Korea Book Corporation
P. O. Box 101, Kwangwhamun
Seoul

KUWAIT
MEMRB
P.O. Box 5465

MALAYSIA
University of Malaya Cooperative Bookshop, Limited
P. O. Box 1127, Jalan Pantai Baru
Kuala Lumpur

MEXICO
INFOTEC
Apartado Postal 22-860
Col. PE/A Pobre
14060 Tlalpan, Mexico D.F.

MOROCCO
Societe d'Etudes Marketing Marocaine
2 Rue Moliere, Bd. d'Anfa
Casablanca

THE NETHERLANDS
Medical Books Europe, BV (MBE)
Noorderwal 38
7241 BL Lochem

NEW ZEALAND
Hills Library and Information Service
Private Bag
New Market
Auckland

NIGERIA
University Press Limited
Three Crowns Building Jericho
Private Mail Bag 5095
Ibadan

NORWAY
Tanum Karl Johan, A.S.
P. O. Box 1177 Sentrum
Oslo 1

PAKISTAN
Mirza Book Agency
65, Shahrah-e-Quaid-e-Azam
P.O. Box No. 729
Lahore 3

PERU
Editorial Desarrollo SA
Apartado 3824
Lima

THE PHILIPPINES
National Book Store
701 Rizal Avenue
Metro Manila

POLAND
ORPAN
Distribution Center for Scientific Publications of the Polish Academy of Sciences
Palac Kultury i Nauki
00-901 WARSZAWA

PORTUGAL
Livraria Portugal
Rua Do Carmo 70-74
1200 Lisbon

SAUDI ARABIA, QATAR
Jarir Book Store
P. O. Box 3196
Riyadh 11471

SINGAPORE, TAIWAN, BURMA, BRUNEI
Information Publications
Private, Ltd.
02-06 1st Fl., Pei-Fu Industrial
Bldg., 24 New Industrial Road
Singapore

SOUTH AFRICA
For single titles
Oxford University Press Southern Africa
P.O. Box 1141
Cape Town 8000

For subscription orders
International Subscription Service
P.O. Box 41095
Craighall
Johannesburg 2024

SPAIN
Mundi-Prensa Libros, S.A.
Castello 37
28001 Madrid

SRI LANKA AND THE MALDIVES
Lake House Bookshop
P.O. Box 244
100, Sir Chittampalam A. Gardiner Mawatha
Colombo 2

SWEDEN
For single titles:
ABCE Fritzes Kungl. Hovbokhandel
Regeringsgatan 12, Box 16356
S-103 27 Stockholm

For Subscription orders:
Wennergren-Williams AB
Box 30004
S-104 25 Stockholm

SWITZERLAND
Librairie Payot
6 Rue Grenus
Case postal 381
CH 1211 Geneva 11

TANZANIA
Oxford University Press
P. O. Box 5299
Dar es Salaam

THAILAND
Central Department Store
306 Silom Road
Bangkok

TRINIDAD & TOBAGO, ANTIGUA, BARBUDA, BARBADOS, DOMINICA, GRENADA, GUYANA, MONTSERRAT, ST. KITTS AND NEVIS, ST. LUCIA, ST. VINCENT & GRENADINES
Systematics Studies Unit
55 Eastern Main Road
Curepe
Trinidad, West Indies

TUNISIA
Societe Tunisienne de Diffusion
5 Avenue de Carthage
Tunis

TURKEY
Haset Kitapevi A.S.
469, Istiklal Caddesi
Beyoglu-Istanbul

UGANDA
Uganda Bookshop
P.O. Box 7145
Kampala

UNITED ARAB EMIRATES
MEMRB Gulf Co.
P. O. Box 6097
Sharjah

UNITED KINGDOM
Microinfo Ltd.
P. O. Box 3
Alton, Hampshire GU 34 2PG
England

VENEZUELA
Libreria del Este
Aptdo. 60.337
Caracas 1060-A

WESTERN SAMOA
Wesley Bookshop
P.O. Box 207
Apia

YUGOSLAVIA
Jugoslovenska Knjiga
YU-11000 Belgrade Trg Republike

ZIMBABWE
Textbook Sales Pvt. Ltd.
Box 3799
Harare